# CUTTING COSTS
## Without
# CUTTING CORNERS

*The Dynamics of Aviation in Nigeria*

Gabriel Olugbenga Olowo

# DEDICATION

This book is dedicated to God and four people I like to describe as my 'destiny helpers': General Muritala Mohammed, Popoola, Soji Amusan and Taiwo Adenekan.

First is General Muritala Mohammed. After I obtained a Higher School Certificate (HSC) in 1973 and there was no funding for my university education, I had to work briefly. While waiting eagerly to complete three years at the then Nigeria Airways Limited where I was working as a flight despatcher trainee and in order to qualify for a staff rebate of N3 ticket to London so as to further my education, the airline restructuring exercise under General Muritala Mohammed as head of state, adopted 'Last-In, First-Out (LIFO)' accounting principle' to surprisingly retire me at an early age of 21. Today, I am grateful for that.

Though frustrated, I succeeded at getting a federal government scholarship to study computer science for an HND degree in the United Kingdom. But questions popped up in my mind about whether I really wanted to pursue an HND since I had decided to work briefly to gather some funds and get a degree either in medicine or engineering. I had studied physics, chemistry and biology at HSC level. I eventually figured that the scholarship would be a distraction.

Secondly, I dedicate this book to Popoola, a friend and colleague of mine at Nigeria Airways who told me he had been invited for an interview as management trainee with Lufthansa German Airlines. Without an invitation, I decided to accompany him to the interview just to try my luck, and as God would have it, I was allowed to join over 200 applicants to take part in an examination for the job which was in three stages of varying difficulties. Regrettably, my friend dropped out at the first stage. At round three, seven of us were selected for an oral interview and I was one of the two eventually selected. This could only have been God's doing and it led me to my fifty years sojourn (till date) in the aviation industry.

This book is also dedicated to Mr. Soji Amusan, the most senior Nigerian in the management hierarchy of Lufthansa German Airline at the time, for not throwing me out of the organization at the completion of the three year programme while reviewing my personnel file and after he discovered I had no application. I confessed that I had only escorted my friend to the examination and 'gate crashed' since no invitation letter was requested before attendees were ushered into the examination room. Providence and capacity had worked for me. Mr. Soji Amusan and myself ended up like twins and as friends (with one older by 10 years) at the University of Lagos for bachelor and master's degree programmes.

Fourthly, I dedicate this book to Mr. Taiwo Adenekan whose voice still speaks, even in death. Adenekan was a junior and a friend both at our cherished Comprehensive High School, Aiyetoro ("Compro") and in the aviation industry. It was Taiwo who first challenged me to put in print a first-class document for would-be aviation practitioners and / or entrepreneurs. His challenge was based on his foresight and witnessing of my growth through the ranks in various aspects of the aviation industry both at home and abroad. It was Taiwo and I (along with Professor Samuel Ekundayo Alao, former president / vice - chancellor of Adeleke University, Ede, Osun State) who started putting the bits and pieces of this book together and here it is today.

# ACKNOWLEDGEMENTS

My appreciation goes to Professor Johnson Egwakhe, the then director of Babcock Centre for Executive Development (BCED) and now group managing director of Babcock Investment Group and his tireless team of individuals who helped to research and tidy up my many interviews, manuscripts, and conference papers.

I also appreciate my spiritual and aviation son, Emmanuel Olusoji Isola, the first vice-president of Sabre Global Technology Limited (SGTL), West Africa, who was instrumental in producing relevant scripts and financial coordination up to the printing stage. I am very grateful to Soji who is always striving to be like me. Thank you!

Most importantly, I thank my darling wife, my best friend, my priest, my prayer partner & prophet, Stella Olubisi Olowo who permanently demonstrates a life filled with the peace of God. The God of Peace saturates our home. We are soaked with amazing grace. YOU ARE CHERISHED!

And to our lovely children (God's heritage) namely Phebe OluwaTomisin Olowo-King, Grace OluwaTomiwo Olowo-Adegboyega, Joshua OluwaTomiyosi Olowo, and Mary OluwaTomisola Olowo-Sokeye, for their consistent love and passion for learning, leadership, discipline, love for God, love of parents, encouragement, and perpetual care. You are all eternally appreciated.

Finally, to our God, immortal and invisible; my Lord and Saviour, Jesus "The Christ," who invited me to come and buy without money. He paid it all and gave me a free gift of salvation, granting me the grace to be in health, in wealth, of a sound mind, serving God, and being a blessing. To Him be glory forever and ever.

Dr. Gabriel Olugbenga Olowo,
2021.

# PREFACE

Countries retain their name and significance in the League of Nations by sustaining each giant stride they make. Aviation was one of the giant strides taken by the Federal Government of Nigeria and within a short time, it became a pride of the nation. The industry did not take time to carve a niche for itself resulting in investors coming in droves to have a stake. For everyone who participated actively during those glory days, the nostalgic feeling will remain a burden. The Nigeria aviation industry is my life, passion, business, pride, and concern. The sky is my home, workplace, and a major focus of my thoughts.

The history of the aviation industry in Nigeria is both challenging and intriguing. This book, though about aviation in Nigeria, is ultimately a story about me: my life, passion, concerns, successes, failures, contributions, and thought-out solutions to problems within the aviation industry in Nigeria. I always ask myself, what and how would I have been without my existence in aviation? I live, walk, work, run and fly in aviation.

In this book, issues of risks, governance, security, information technology, telecommunications, ticket/ airway bill, crew, airline failures and capitalization matters affecting the aviation industry are explored. The book also covers issues relating to operators, regulators, travelers and media who are all stakeholders in the aviation industry. Interestingly, it was a statement from a friend during a golf playing time at Ikeja that sparked this interest and ignited my analytic mind to reflect on my earlier days in the Nigeria aviation industry. "Like yesterday," as my mother would say, "My son has become a man" I still see the aviation industry like a mother looking at her toddler moving into full adulthood despite all the challenges associated with growth.

I will liken my experience in aviation to the human body which has different sensory organs. My perspectives, experiences and observations in this industry cut across its many parts. Like a typical story of a human being, there were years of celebration, boom, bumps, and tears that raised nagging questions ('which way Nigeria?'). There were moments when life played out like a game and the only spectator happened to be myself. There were also days when too many questions demanded answers but the answers were as elusive as rain in the dry season. I have had hours when minutes would seem like years and time just didn't pass quickly enough. Yet, despite all the challenges, the aviation industry has remained the industry I love.

At Ikeja where the challenging statement was made, my mind went to a lot of things including how impressionable my mind was when I was much younger. I can remember how when I looked up, I could see how the birds made way for the arrival of the 'flying white man's car'. I thought the plane was a kind of car that could fly. I thought the flying car was one that required a special place to park; executive stairs and steps to walk- down and had wonderful people to show you where to sit inside. I thought this special car belonged to a few wealthy people.

During my childhood, I saw planes flying over my village and I used to trace them with my fingers until they disappeared in the clouds. What never crossed my mind then was that one day I would not only be flying in them but also dedicating my working life and like now, writing a book about them. I have not written this book because I am the most knowledgeable about the aviation industry but because I have been an active player in it and feel a sense of responsibility to share my experiences, thoughts, observations and solutions with every reader. Like a mother telling her children stories of what was, is and to come, I tell the history of Nigeria aviation from what was, is and the way forward.

I remember my youthful years being full of flying kites, school excursions to airports with parked planes and their large tires, extended wings on their sides, dirty tails and unfriendly take off sounds piercing into the ears. In my adult life, I entered the world of planes as a traveler, pilot, engineer, and witnessed ugly sights of plane crashes and participated in rescue efforts. These memories and experiences are the reasons for my concern regarding the future of the Nigeria aviation industry and my quest for a long-term strategy to give it a competitive edge amongst her contemporaries in Africa. This deep concern has stayed subconsciously in my thoughts and has been noticeable enough to the extent that even my son, when watching me one day, said, "Father, you look so keen and worried, what bothers you so much?" I replied, "Aviation, Nigerian aviation." This got him curious and he suddenly followed up with a barrage of questions: "What about it? Can you please share these challenges with me? What are the prospects and potentials of the aviation industry? What is the history of the industry in Nigeria?" As these questions were coming out from a young Nigerian seeking for answers, it occurred to me that there are millions of Nigerians who are grappling with the same questions in their minds. After my son's questions sank in, I said to him, "Well son, before I detail the history of the aviation industry in Nigeria, permit me to state unequivocally that, the major challenge of the industry in Nigeria is the 'cutting costs and cutting corner' syndrome."

Meanwhile, the right approach which is in line with international best practices is, '**Cutting Costs without Cutting Corners**.' It is the mismatch between these opposite ideas that has put the industry in a quagmire. Enthroning the right policies, setting up the structures, maintaining professionalism and promoting enabling business environment was all that we needed to take the lead. It was a question of aligning all the dimensions properly such that, at the pull of a string, all the parts would respond immediately. Nigeria's aviation industry, based on the county's numerous endowments, has the potential to be a market leader with others coming in far distance behind. The potential is still there, what was lacking and is still lacking today is the unlocking of this potential through understanding of the dynamics.

This book has fifteen chapters. Chapter one deals with the history of aviation generally with the experiences of Nigeria discussed extensively. Chapter two is about aviation risk management. It explores the position of Nigerian aviation in risk management. Chapter three is about travel agents and travel management companies. These constitute an allimportant sector in the aviation value chain. Chapter four discusses issues of corporate governance which is the bane of Nigeria's aviation industry. In chapter five, regulations and policy implementation is presented to showcase the role of different regulatory organizations in the aviation industry. Chapter six contains the history and development of civil aviation regulations detailing the reasons behind the establishment of all the civil aviation regulation agencies. In chapter seven, logistics issues are examined and chapter eight is about crew management in Nigeria's aviation industry explaining the role of onboard staff in the industry. Chapter nine explores customer care as they are not always treated well by airline operators. Chapter ten considers accounting and cost reduction against compromise in aviation industry.

In chapter eleven, profit maximization is explained while chapter twelve introduces safety and ground maintenance issues, stressing all the safety precautions that need to take place anytime an aircraft lands in an airport before the next flight. Chapter thirteen looks into innovative technologies in the aviation industry and how they work. Chapter fourteen and fifteen are about safety management and security management in aviation respectively, emphasizing the roles of staff training and management for optimum performance and enhanced productivity. All chapters are knitted with relevant case studies.

# FOREWORD

The book, *"Cutting Costs without Cutting Corners," Aviation in Nigeria - The Dynamics, i*s a timely contribution to the discourse on entrenchment of international best practices in Nigeria's aviation industry ninety-six years after the first airplane landed in the ancient city of Kano. This historic event that later gave rise to a booming industry with the Nigeria Airways leading and setting pace for many other carriers in the continent remains significant. The following failure of the national carrier which was as a result of poor corporate governance, frequent government interference and other societal ills was phenomenal and continues to manifest as an Internal Mechanism Deficiency Syndrome (IMDS) affecting the entire aviation industry up till the present time, making it impossible for an average airline to thrive even in the midst of huge aviation market.

This book is an insider perspective and a contribution to the discussion on the aviation industry business especially touching on the "hornet's nest" of the precarious nature of the industry in Nigeria. It will be wrong to claim ignorance of the negative happenings in the industry. It will be worse to act as though one is a mere spectator or to encourage it through inaction having witnessed firsthand, the negative outcomes which could have been averted. Therefore, this book is a handy pathfinder for the nation's quest to realizing the dynamics of operating a modern-day aviation industry suitable for the teeming air travelling public in Nigeria.

Realizing that the airplane is the fastest and safest means of transportation which is important in connecting people, transforming society, building values and generally, laying the foundation for all phases and facets of development, makes a book such as this, a welcome development.

This book projects the undeniably significant position and roles of the aviation industry globally in both developed and developing countries. Predominantly, it draws attention to the situation in Nigeria where the national carrier had the misfortune of liquidation after having a total of ten managing directors within a space of ten years. The private commercial airlines that came into the market have, unfortunately, not optimally benefited from the huge potentials available in the aviation industry.

This book also underlines the great contribution of ICAO, the American FAA, EASA and others in the area of formulating and enforcing safety regulations. It has also recognized IATA Operational Safety Audit, (IOSA), and the enthronement of a safety culture in the implementation of Safety Management System (SMS) across the entire industry from the regulator, to the service providers and the airlines.

An important merit of this book is its focus on historical narratives thereby providing useful information on the first airplane that landed in Nigeria, the birth of Nigeria Airways and the era of private commercial airline operators. Much of the information given in this book may hitherto be unknown to many people within the aviation industry. For instance, the author believes that most of the commercial airlines in Nigeria are facing challenges operating strictly in accordance with the existing regulations even though they are aware of the consequences of their actions or inactions. This book highlights the friction between the task- masters and the owners of airline businesses. Since it is said that, he who "pays the piper dictates the tune," they (airline owners) wield an over bearing influence on the taskmasters (managers) who must comply in order to keep their jobs even when it will involve cutting corners.

The mission of the author, which is to launch a discourse on the internationally acceptable methods of cutting costs in aviation business without cutting corners, has been clearly met. The methodology adopted by the author is data driven and one is able to identify the critical role which the aviation industry has played and is still playing in Nigeria. It is significant to note the case study approach is used in this book to buttress the point that most commercial airlines in Nigeria are not economically viable and buoyant as a result of low fares, the ownership structure and size of the aircraft deployed. Several findings are eloquently discussed and the recommendations thereof have been aptly captured in the chapters of the book.

The author, Dr. Gbenga Olowo, has brought his wealth of experience to bear in this reference piece. It was his yearning to pursue a career in aviation right from childhood and this dream has been fulfilled as his social mobility got him through to serve as the head of one of the defunct airlines in Nigeria among many other experiences. Thus, the book, *Cutting Costs without Cutting Corners in Aviation in Nigeria: The Dynamics* is the author's personal account of what transpired in the course of his trainings, working and leadership in the aviation industry. Written in a straightforward prose, there are several case studies which add credence to the different subjects discussed.

'Cutting Costs Without Cutting Corners' is for everyone. Policy formulators, airline owners and operators will benefit from reading it, as well as general readers. The air travelling community, staff and relevant stakeholders in the aviation industry will find it instructive, and the global community will find it a mine of information. It is a book that everyone in the aviation sector should read as we continue to explore the modalities of cutting costs in the aviation industry without cutting corners.

This book should be a compulsory reading for all and I, therefore, highly recommend it to anyone who is interested in understanding the dynamics of aviation industry in Nigeria and the snags that have slowed and mutilated the sector making it to underperform when compared with other African nations.

Dr. Harold Demuren
Former DG – Nigeria Civil Aviation Authority (NCAA)

# TABLE OF CONTENTS

DEDICATION ............................................................... ii

ACKNOWLEDGEMENTS ............................................. iv

PREFACE ................................................................... v

FOREWORD ............................................................ ix

**CHAPTER ONE**
AVIATION IN NIGERIA: A BIRD'S EYE VIEW ..................................... 1

**CHAPTER TWO**
AVIATION RISK MANAGEMENT: WHERE ARE WE? .................................. 24

**CHAPTER THREE**
TRAVEL AGENT AND TRAVEL MANAGEMENT COMPANY (TMC) - MOLUE
(MASS TRANSIT BUS) MENTALITY............................................. 46

**CHAPTER FOUR**
CORPORATE GOVERNANCE: THE MISSING LINK....................................... 52

**CHAPTER FIVE**
REGULATION AND POLICY IMPLEMENTATION: THE ROLE OF
GOVERNMENT AND POLICY EFFECTIVENESS.......................................... 65

**CHAPTER SIX**
HISTORY AND DEVELOPMENT OF CIVIL AVIATION REGULATIONS: THE
NIGERIAN EXPERIENCE ......................................................... 70

**CHAPTER SEVEN**
LOGISTICS: HIPPOS AND GAZELLES............................................. 80

**CHAPTER EIGHT**
CREW MANAGEMENT IN THE NIGERIAN AVIATION INDUSTRY................ 97

**CHAPTER NINE**
CUSTOMER CARE: THE CHALLENGE....................................... 105

**CHAPTER TEN**
ACCOUNTING: COST REDUCTION VS. COMPROMISE ............................ 115

**CHAPTER ELEVEN**
PROFIT MAXIMIZATION: ETHICS AND PROFIT ....................................... 128

**CHAPTER TWELVE**
SAFETY AND GROUND MAINTENANCE: FLYING COFFINS ...................... 145

**CHAPTER THIRTEEN**
INNOVATIVE TECHNOLOGY: THE PARADOX .......................................... 161

**CHAPTER FOURTEEN**
SAFETY MANAGEMENT: THE NIGERIAN AVIATION STORY .................... 174

**CHAPTER FIFTEEN**
SECURITY MANAGEMENT: GAPS AND OUR EXPERIENCES .................... 183

**EPILOGUE** .............................................................................. 202

**REFERENCE** ........................................................................... 207

**JOURNALS** ............................................................................. 210

**BOOKS** ................................................................................... 212

# CHAPTER ONE

# AVIATION IN NIGERIA:
## A Bird's Eye View

Aviation is the fastest, safest and most convenient means of transportation in the world. It can be said to have existed far beyond two thousand years. It began in its earliest form as kites flying in an attempt to jump the tower, then to hypersonic and finally lighterthan- air jets.

In the year 1901 A.D., Alberto Santos-Dumont announced his first take-off machine or what is called air-strip named Number 6. The machine or air-strip flew for thirty (30) minutes over Paris and the Eiffel Tower. Alberto was known as a substantive designer and builder of several kinds of aircrafts. As at 1908, he began working with the Clement – Bayard Company to build the de Moiselle No 19 which was recorded as the world's first produced mass aircraft. The use of airship or air-movement machine(s) gained much awareness during and after the First and Second World Wars. For the commercial aviation sector, the Concorde Passenger Jet made room for the emergence of airlines such as British Airways which was the foremost national and international airline in pioneering activities for commercial aviation services.

The history of Aviation in Nigeria revolves around the various phases of challenges and successes that the industry has gone through and or is still going through. As an industry, aviation occupies a strategic position such that it has indeed become indispensable for the socio-economic development of any nation, especially Nigeria judging from its economic and political significance. The aviation industry started in Nigeria as a baby of the British colonial government.

The aviation story in Nigeria can be traced back to November 1, 1925 in the traditional, commercial, and ancient walled city of Kano, when the first aircraft landed. According to John and John (2019) there was an incident that created tension between the British colonialists and the residents of Kano. On sensing that the issue might get out of control, the authorities in London promptly instructed the commanding officer of the Khartoum RAF Squadron to fly to Kano and deal with the circumstances head-on. The Bristol fighter plane landed on the Horse Race Course ground popularly known as the Polo Club in Kano at about 5.20pm. This event, for Kano in particular and Nigeria at large, marked a historic milestone in the then socio-economic, political and commercial landscape of Nigeria. One could have unmistakably forecasted that the first aircraft to land in Nigeria would have been in Lagos, because Lagos was Nigeria's seat of power for the British Colonial government and commanded significant influx of human traffic. Interestingly, that status has not changed as Lagos still maintains its status as the commercial nerve centre of Nigeria. The specific reason behind the aircraft landing in Kano is not very clear, but it is alleged that it landed in Kano because a top colonial authority had made a stopover from London. Significantly, without air routes, maps or radio communication, the plane safely landed. Regardless of the feat, the landing was regarded as "a hazardous operation" nevertheless, it gave rise to subsequent flight drops from Cairo, Egypt for the Royal Air-force (RAF). The landing of this plane was spectacular and monumental so much so that a Kano resident was moved to capture this peculiar scene through an art painting that served as a reference master piece. The "water colour picture" was later acquired by the government. Meanwhile, the RAF landing operation would later become a yearly event, while the route was also extended to Maiduguri and thereafter, to other parts of the country.

## 1. THE FIRST NIGERIAN PILOTS

At the early stages of agitation for liberation from colonialism, Haye, a boy born in one of the villages in what is now Delta State, was keenly interested in becoming a pilot. He picked up the interest for flying while watching the Royal Marine Officers on duty in Sapele in the early 1950s. He wanted to be like them. After attending a series of interviews meant to determine eligibility for training, three Nigerians were granted scholarship. They were Bob Hayes, Joseph Ajakaiye and Samuel Ohioma.

On August 9, 1953, these three young Nigerians left our shores for training as the first set of Nigerian pilots at the Flying School, Hamble, Southampton, England. About five years before Nigeria's independence, precisely in May 1955, Bob Hayes, at the age of 20 years, became the first Nigerian to get certified as a pilot with a commercial pilot license. He returned to Nigeria and joined the West African Airways Corporation (WAAC). From 1956 to 1960, this young Nigerian pilot flew as a co-pilot on local routes and as at 1962, he began flying on international routes. Captain Bob Hayes was the first Nigerian pilot to fly into New York City. He, later in his career, served as acting managing director of the defunct national carrier, the Nigeria Airways Limited. During his active service, Hayes supervised, trained and mentored many pilots in Nigeria until his retirement in 1990, having accomplished the compulsory 35 years in service. After retirement, he worked on contract as a training captain and examiner. Captain Bob Hayes was the first Nigerian pilot to put in more than 40 years of service in the Nigeria aviation industry. With time, a female pilot emerged to the surprise of many who felt piloting was an exclusive career for men. She was Chinyere Onyenucheya, the first female pilot in Nigeria.

The Nigerian aviation industry is actually a by-product of the British colonial government. With the phenomenal aircraft landing in 1925, the door for more players was opened.

According to Vincent Orange Coningham, the era of commercial aviation gradually began to set in. The foremost recorded commercial aviation activity in Nigeria was attributed to a man called Bob Carpenter. He owned a light aircraft referred to as De Havilland Moth. This aircraft was among the first types of aircraft.

As recorded, he frequently undertook high-risk flights to and from Kano and Lagos, using the rail track as his guide. Also, in the early 1930s, an enterprising pilot shuttled a few fare-paying passengers in a sea plane to and from Lagos and Warri.

As regional long-haul flights continued, aviation activities in Nigeria began to develop, which brought about the need for aerodromes (Federal Airport Authority of Nigeria, Airport Operations, 2016). Before this time, the business of flying was monopolized by the British. Thereafter, British Overseas Airways Corporation (BOAC) dovetailed into West African Airways Corporation (WAAC). Subsequently, representatives of the Air Ministry in London visited Nigeria to inspect what could be described as appropriate landing ground sites in Kano, Kaduna, Maiduguri, Minna, Lagos and Oshogbo.

Within a space of one year (1935-1936), the air traffic operations being carried out by Royal Air Force (RAF), was substituted by Imperial Airways with its major operations of flying mails and passengers from London to Nigeria. It also included other routes, such as flying from Cairo to Uganda, and Khartoum to Nigeria.

With more enlightenment, air transportation gained good reputation amongst the elites, as the fastest means of transportation, especially for long distance journeys. Thus, both public and private investors began to express interest in investing in the aviation industry. The King of England on May 1946 established the West African Air Transport Authority (WAATA). This group consisted of the governors of Nigeria, Gold Coast (Ghana), Sierra Leone and the Gambia, with the governor of Nigeria serving as the president. Eventually, the West African Airways Corporation (WAAC), which operated from 1946 to 1958, was established by these same countries with the mandate to develop air services in and between West African territories. The headquarters for the airways was in Ikeja, Lagos, Nigeria. Lagos also served as the operating hub and the airline began her operations with a six-seater De-Havilland Dave Aircraft. Nigeria's domestic services operated with the dove as the west coast service, making use of the Bristol warfare. The management of this civil directorate of public works of these countries and their legislative authority was a prototype of the United Kingdom Colonial Air Navigator Order (UKCANO).

As WAAC member countries attained independence, Ghana in 1957, began to pull out of the coalition and this led to the dissolution of WAAC.

However, with the dissolution of WAAC on September 30, 1958, the Nigerian government in partnership with the British Overseas Air Cooperation (BOAC) and Elder Dempster Lines formed the WAAC-Nigeria which eventually metamorphosed into Nigeria Airways. The name WAAC was retained due to the image and prestige the company earned in the past as a joint effort between four former British West

African colonies (Akpoghomeh, 1999). This single but historic occurrence heralded the genesis of the airline industry in Nigeria. Thus, by implication, the Nigeria Airways from inception comprised of a tripartite ownership both in governance and shareholders' structure. The Nigeria government owned 51% share, Elder Dempster Lines 32%, and British Overseas Airways Corporation (BOAC) 17% (Flight international, 1958, 1960 and 2003).

WAAC-Nigeria inherited some aircrafts previously owned by WAAC and the operation commenced on October 1st, 1958 (a year after Ghana got her independence and pulled out) and two years before Nigerian independence in 1960. There was also a BOAC Stratocruiser VC 10 that was linking London with Lagos (Flight International, 1958b). A fifteen (15) year contract agreement was signed with BOAC to charter the Stratocruiser and Britannia for servicing long – haul flights between Nigeria and the United Kingdom.

On March 25, 1961, Nigeria became the sole owner of the company as both Elder Dempster and BOAC sold their shares to the Nigerian government (Guttery, 1998) and the wholly owned Nigerian airline was renamed, 'Nigeria Airways Limited.'

The Nigeria Airways enjoyed flourishing operations, although with various phases of development and peculiar crisis, until the year 2003 when the operation was put on hold, having operated for 45 years. Nigeria Airways did so well that it was the first African Airline to acquire a terminal in the United States at John F. Kennedy International Airport (JFK) (Ejuka, 1987). It did not suffer lack of funds, markets, well trained manpower, equipment or enabling environment (Olakunle, 2000).

The news of its stoppage came as shocking and heart breaking to people like Mr. Peter Gana the then CEO and to Nigerians as a whole. This occurred when the Nigeria Airways which used to parade about 30 fleet of aircrafts declined to just one feeble operational aircraft but had sufficient assets in spares, engines, estates, offices and subsidiaries good enough to sustain and rebrand operations with new ownership and different goals & objectives for a viable operation.

The various assets were recommended by experts to be stripped to form subsidiary companies including Skypower Handling Company (Sahcol), Skypower Catering (on board catering), Skypower Water, Skypower Maintenance and Repair Organisation, Skypower Estates, etc. Income streams from these subsidiaries were to be used to revive and sustain a viable airline operation and retain manpower. Forensic audit of inventories and staff was concluded and staff rationalization based on the planned new fleet was being concluded for the new national carrier rebirth, when a rather absurd decision that was not properly articulated was taken by government and the airline was liquidated with all its assets prodigally sold by government.

Whereas the new national airline was to be repackaged and sold to the public, the huge consequences of the liquidation particularly labor issues, remain naughty till date. Many devoted Nigerians who spent their careers in the organization, died untimely. It was indeed a very gory and sad ending for a one-time flourishing national pride, no thanks to civilians in military democracy.

Before then, many experts were assembled (including this author) to serve in the ministerial committee that was to chart the above new path for the airline. The author was privileged to be part of the committee for restructuring of the airline but the committee's report was discarded as of no consequence. National carrier rebirth (aka Nigeria Airways) remains a mirage as at the time of this writing.

## 2. AIRLINE CRASHES IN NIGERIA

Despite the progress recorded by the industry, it also suffered a lot of set-backs, most of which could be traced to lack of adequate managerial capability and accountability resulting from lack of grounded analytical competency in the quest for cutting costs. The obsession with cutting costs can, to a large extent, be linked to the series of air crashes, some of which could have been averted if operations were appropriately and properly guided. The account of airline crashes in Nigeria generally has been mostly tragic and the casualty rate seems to make it the deadliest means of transportation, more than any other form of transportation in the world. According to Andrew and Paul (2015), deaths recorded in air crashes are more than any other form of transportation in the world, but the state of emergency-responses to air mishaps in Nigeria is abysmal to say the least. A quick look at the table below will buttress this point further as it shows the amount of air accidents and casualties recorded.

| Airline | Place of Incidence | Date | Casualties |
| --- | --- | --- | --- |
| Nigeria Airways BAC VC10 | Lagos | November 20, 1969 | 87 people |
| Royal Jordanian Airlines flight 70 | Kano | January 22, 1973 | 176 people |
| Nigeria Airways, F28-1000 | Kano | March 1, 1978 | 16 People |
| Nigeria Airways F28-1000 | Near Enugu | November 28, 1983 | 53 people |
| Sky Power Brandeironate Aircraft | Ilorin Airport runway | December 1988 | All passengers |

| | | | |
|---|---|---|---|
| Okada Air BAC-111 | Sokoto | June 26, 1990 | 6 people injured |
| British Helicopter | Eket, Akwa Ibom | February 24,1991 | 9 people |
| Cessna Citation 550 of Ashaka Cement | Gombe | May 21, 1991 | All on board |
| Okada Air BA-111 | Sokoto | June 26, 1991 | 3 people |
| Nigeria Airways DC 8-61 | Jeddah Saudi Arabia | July 11, 1991 | 261 people |
| Nigeria Air force AC-130 | Lagos, | September 26, 1992 | 200 people |
| A Harka Airlines Soviet-era Tupolev Tu | Lagos | June 25, 1995 | 16 people |
| Nigeria Airways Boeing 737-2F9 | Kaduna | November 13, 1995 | 9 people |
| British Hawker Siddeley 125 jet | Kano | January 17, 1996 | 14 people |
| Airline Boeing 727-23 | Lagos | November 7, 1996 | 151 people |
| Sky Power Express Airways Embrear 110IA | Yola, | January 31, 1997 | 5 people |
| NAF Dornier 228-212 | Nguru, Bornu | September 12, 1997 | 10 people |
| Sky Power Express | Airways Abuja, | January 5, 2000 | 17 people |
| Bandeirante 110IA Dornier aircraft | Niger Delta | October 26, 2000 | 6 injured |

| | | | |
|---|---|---|---|
| EAS Airlines BAC 1-11 500 | Kano | May 4, 2002 | 148 people |
| Hydro Cargo Brussets, Belgium | Lagos | November 30, 2003 | Crash landed |
| Aenail Spray Aircraft, Nigeria Ltd | Barfreex Bauchi Airport | March 6, 2004 | Nil |
| Pan African Airline's Helicopter | Escravos, Delta State | July 26, 2004 | 4 people |
| Boeing 727 of Chanchangi Airlines | MMA Yola Airport | December 29, 2004 | Nil |
| Kenya Airlines Aircraft | MMA Yola Airport | December 29, 2004 | Nil |
| Nigeria Air Force Fighter | Kano | January 28, 2005 | Nil |
| ADC's B73 aircraft | Yola Airport | February 25, 2005 | Nil |
| Boeing 737 of Belleview | Lagos | March 27, 2005 | Nil |
| Domestic Chachangi Airlines, Boeing 727-200 aircraft | Lagos | June 11/12, 2005 | Nil |
| Another overshot their runway at airport | Jos | June 10, 2005 | Nil |
| Russian aircraft, Belonging to Harka Air | MMA Yola Airport | June 24, 2005 | All on board |
| Air France A330 | Port Harcourt | July 6, 2005 | Only cows |
| Lufthansa Aircraft | Lagos Airport | July 23, 2005 | Nil |

| | | | |
|---|---|---|---|
| Belleview Airplane, Boeing 737 Airliner | Lagos | October 22, 2005 | 117 people |
| Soliso Airlines DC-9 18-Seater Dornier 228 Air for Transport Plane | Port Harcourt | December 10, 2005 | 103 people |
| Plane with Registration Number 228–212 | Oko Village, Benue State. | September 17, 2006 | 15 people |
| Aviation Development Corporation Airline, Boeing 737 | Abuja's Airport | October 29, 2006 | 98 people |
| OAS Service Helicopter | Warri, Delta State | November 10, 2006 | 4 people |
| Bristow Owned Helicopter | ExxonMobil Facility in Port Harcourt | August 2, 2007 | 1 person |
| Beech Craft 1900 Plane Marked 5N- JAH | Obudu Airstrip, Cross River | March 15 2008 | 4 people |
| Helicopter Belonging to Joint Task Force | Kabong, Jos | March 14, 2002 | All On Board |
| Airline Services (EAS) BAC-1-11-525F1 | Kano | May 4, 2002 | 70 people |
| Sosoliso Airlines Flight 1145 | Port Harcourt | Dec. 10, 2005 | 109 people |

| | | | |
|---|---|---|---|
| A twin Engine Boeing 737 | Ogun State | Oct. 22, 2005 | 117 people |
| ADC Aircraft | Abuja | Oct. 29, 2006 | 105 people |
| Six-Seater Helicopter Belonging to Odengene Air Shuttle (OAS) | Delta State | Nov. 10, 2006 | 2 people |
| Air Force Plane | Benue State | Sept. 16, 2006 | 12 people |
| A Twin-Turbo Prop 19- Seater Aircraft Belonging to Wings Aviation Limited | Calabar | March 15, 2008 | 4 people |
| HS-125 Chartered Aircraft | Bauchi | March 8, 2011 | Nil |
| Kwara State- Bound Helicopter | Osun State | July 29, 2011 | 4 people |
| Nigerian Police Aircraft | Jos | March 14, 2012 | 3 people |
| Dana Air Flight | Iju-Ishaga, Lagos | June 3, 2012 | 170 people |
| Kaduna State Helicopter | Jos | Dec. 15, 2012 | 5 people |
| DHV 111 Cargo Aircraft, Nigeria | Accra, Ghana | June 2, 2012 | 10 people |
| BELL Helicopter 206 | Opebi, Ikeja, Lagos | August 28, 2020 | 2 people |

While this list is not exhaustive, it speaks volumes about the precarious nature of our aviation industry. The pendulum does not swing to any side, both government and passenger aircrafts were all ill-fated. The missing link is centered on altering the basic economics of aviation business by the owners, whether in public or private sector. Often, there is a halo-effect that allows for the involvement of family members, close associates, friends and acquaintances in the running and management of a complex industry like aviation. This has been the grievous mistake repeatedly made. Why must we place ego and personal interests over and above the life of millions of people who depend on aviation services? Every time there is a mishap, the entire world turns to the men in positions of authority, believing that they must have answers to the yearnings of the general public. From the manufacturers, to the different regulatory bodies (local and international), people want to know what could have gone wrong?

To their chagrin, the immediate result has been absolute silence. Of course, there are people in management positions, but, they are "figures" without "force" and men without authority. They take instructions from the owners who most often know little about airline dynamics. Hence, entrenchment of command-and-control mentality which slows down decision making efforts and because this is concealed from the public eye, the reality becomes the case of treacherous path, with land mines, time-bombs and selfdestructive devises buried under the earth which are bound to detonate with time. Though there are incidents that are regarded as "acts of God", some of the unfortunate aircraft mishaps would not have happened had the owners allowed experts and professionals the freedom to set up and manage the airline businesses in accordance with regulations that are in line with global best practices.

One dangerous trait that I have identified is that of "I-know-it-all" by the airline owners. This trait is responsible for the circumvention of critical regulatory rules and requirements on both the aircraft and manpower. The task-owner whose stake is his employment, is undervalued, unrecognized, and disregarded since the ownermanager calls all the shots.

Thus, Nigeria Airways was killed partly because of mismanagement but principally by 'powers at the top' – the culture of the 'owner' dictating what he/she wants without any reference or regard to professionals who know the intricacies of airline operations.

By the way, the professional is that man or woman competent and skilled in one or more specific activity in a trade rather than a past time. 'Ordinary' airline ticket which is a contract document of carriage between the airline and the passenger requires a lot of skill to conclude unlike many other tickets. Ditto air worthiness requires special skills to ascertain and cannot be handled with triviality. Aviation engages diverse professionals.

Inherent works of the quality control systems are often overlooked and operation manual becomes a mere decor in the museum or library of many airlines. Air trip documentations, human reports and voyage log books that need to be routinely completed to enable engineers ascertain real time operational status of the aircraft are either ignored or completed with wrong information, all in the quest to cut corners for the purpose of maximizing gain.

## 3. AVIATION AUTHORITY

### The Nigeria Civil Aviation Authority (NCAA)

Even though the aviation industry has been gaining stability with the passage of time, it has also faced some challenges that cannot be swept under the carpet. These challenges led to the need and demand for a regulatory authority. As a result of the obvious instabilities, the Nigeria Civil Aviation Authority (NCAA) was created by decree 49 of 1999 among others. It was saddled with the special statutory responsibility that includes regulating, monitoring, and promoting safety and security, to ensure economic growth and sustain reliability for the aviation industry. NCAA was expected to carry out this responsibility in accordance with International Civil Aviation Organization's (ICAO) Standard and Recommended Practices (SARPs).

On January 1, 2000, NCAA commenced operation fully and effectively as a constituted authority. Before 1989, the Civil Aviation Department (CAD) of the Federal Ministry of Aviation had carried out the responsibilities given to the NCAA and the provision of Air Traffic Services. Prior to the acceptance of national policies on civil aviation of 1988 by the federal government, the Federal Civil Aviation Authority (FCAA) was established under decree 8 of 1990 as a regulatory authority for Nigeria's aviation sector. The body succeeded CAD.

In order to further strengthen the aviation sector, in the last quarter of 1995, a decision was taken to re-organize some major government parastatals in the aviation sector. This led to the scrapping of FCAA. New directorates of safety regulation and monitoring, economic regulation and monitoring were established in the Federal Ministry of Aviation to operate in place of the scrapped FCAA. Air traffic services, Aerotel Department and the Nigeria Aviation Authority were merged to form the Federal Airport Authority of Nigeria (FAAN).

The Nigeria Civil Aviation Authority (NCAA) is the certified regulatory entity for the aviation sector in Nigeria. It was backed by law to become autonomous via the civil aviation Act 2006 by the National Assembly. The entity was not just to regulate airline safety but to carry oversight functions on the airlines, airport, airspace, meteorological services as well as the economic regulation of the industry. NCAA operates with seven directorates and service units including ICT, legal, audit and media.

The directorates include:

A. **Flight Standards Group (FSG) Directorates:** The Flight Standards Group is a unit in the Nigeria Civil Aviation Authority (NCAA) that warehouses four other directorates which carry out related safety responsibilities. The directorates under Flight Standards Group are:

1. Directorate of Operations & Training (DOT)
2. Directorate of Airworthiness Standards (DAWS)
3. Directorate of Licensing (DOL)
4. Department of Aeromedical Services (DAMS)

B. **Directorate of Airworthiness Standards (DAWS):** is saddled with the sole responsibility of ensuring the airworthiness of aircrafts in Nigeria. That is, ensuring "Fit-to- Fly aircrafts."

C. **DAWS** also schedules inspection and certification of aircrafts. It supervises the Nigeria aviation industry in order to ensure compliance with global contemporary aviation trends and recommends corrective procedures to ensure air safety.

D. **Directorate of Licensing (DOL):** The Directorate of Licensing is responsible for the licensing of all personnel within the Nigeria Civil Aviation Industry in line with ICAO Annex 1 Standards and Recommended Practices (SARPs).

E. Directorate of Operations and Training (DOT): **The** Directorate of Operations and Training (DOT) ensures effective and efficient activities and setting of standards for flight operations and training of crews in the Nigeria air transport industry.

F. **Directorate of Aerodrome and Airspace Standards (DAAS):** The major responsibility of this sub-unit is to checkmate safety and security and also ensure conformity with the required standards and recommendations of the ICAO Annexes.

G. **Directorate of Finance and Administration:** They are responsible for the formulation of policies towards effective and efficient service delivery, and also to coordinate and manage the financial, administrative, human resources, corporate affairs / planning of the Nigeria Civil Aviation Authority (NCAA).

H. **The Directorate of Consumer Protection Department (CPD):** This department was created in March 2001, to satisfy all aviation consumers with the best obtainable services in air transportation.

I. **The Directorate of Air Transport Regulation (DATR):** They are saddled with a statutory responsibility of managing safety and economic related issues of the civil aviation industry. This has to be in accordance with the provisions of Part IX Section 30 (7a) of the Civil Aviation Act 2006, NCAA Website, NCAR (Nig CARs) 2006).

With this well-structured civil aviation system, the Nigerian civil aviation industry is one of Africa's most flourishing aviation industries. Also, the sector plays a pivotal role in the transportation system of Nigeria. Gravitating towards the socio-economic potentials of the country, the sector can boast of about 28 airports located in various parts of the country of which five are functioning internationally and the other 23 are serving the domestic routes.

Below is the list of airports and their locations in Nigeria.

Furthermore, the industry can also boast of about 554 licensed pilots, 913 licensed engineers, 1700 cabin personnel, 490 well- trained air traffic controllers and about 22 foreign carriers. Nigeria also has a Bilateral Air Services Agreement (BASA) agreement with over 78 countries.

# 4. LIST OF THE AIRPORTS AND THEIR LOCATIONS IN NIGERIA

| City Served | State | ICAO (Int'l Civil Aviation | IATA (Int'l Air Transport Asso.) | Airport Name |
|---|---|---|---|---|
| **International Airports** | | | | |
| Abuja | FCT | DNAA | ABV | Nnamdi Azikiwe International Airport |
| Enugu | Enugu | DNEN | ENU | Akanu Ibiam International Airport |
| Ilorin | Kwara | DNIL | ILR | Ilorin International Airport |
| Kaduna | Kaduna | DNKA | KAD | Kaduna International Airport |
| Kano | Kano | DNKN | KAN | Mallam Aminu Kano International Airport |
| Lagos | Lagos | DNMM | LOS | Murtala Muhammed International Airport |
| Port Harcourt | Rivers | DNPO | PHC | Port Harcourt International Airport |
| Sokoto | Sokoto | DNSO | SKO | Sadiq Abubakar III International Airport |

| Major Domestic Airports | | | | |
|---|---|---|---|---|
| Asaba | Delta | DNAS | ABB | Asaba International Airport |
| Bauchi | Bauchi | DNBC | BCU | Sir Abubakar Tafawa Balewa Airport |
| Benin | Edo | DNBE | BNI | Benin Airport |
| Calabar | Cross River | DNCA | CBQ | Margaret Ekpo International Airport |
| Ibadan | Oyo | DNIB | IBA | Ibadan Airport |
| Jos | Plateau | DNJO | JOS | Yakubu Gowon Airport |
| Maid uguri | Borno | DNMA | MIU | Maiduguri International Airport |
| Owerri | Imo | DNIM | QOW | Sam Mbakwe International Cargo Airport |
| Uyo | Akwa Ibom | DNAI | QUO | Akwa Ibom International Airport |
| Yola | Adamawa | DNYO | YOL | Yola Airport |
| | | | | |

## Other Domestic Airports

| | | | | |
|---|---|---|---|---|
| Akure | Ondo | DNAK | AKR | Akure Airport |
| Bauchi | Bauchi | DNBA | | Bauchi Airport |
| Birnin Kebbi | Kebbi | DNBK | | Kebbi International Airport |
| Dutse | Jigawa | DNDS | | Dutse International Airport |
| Jalingo | Taraba | DNJA | | Jalingo Airport |
| Katsina | Katsina | DNKT | DKA | Katsina Airport |
| Makurdi | Benue | DNMK | MDI | Makurdi Airport |
| Minna | Niger | DNMN | MXJ | Minna Airport |
| Warri | Delta | DNSU | QRW | Warri Airport |
| Yenagoa | Bayelsa | | | Bayelsa International Airport |
| Zaria | Kaduna | DNZA | ZAR | Zaria Airport |

## Other Airports Not Owned / Managed by FAAN

| | | | | |
|---|---|---|---|---|
| Uyo | Akwa Ibom | DNAI | QUO | Akwa Ibom Airport |

## Airstrips

| | | | | |
|---|---|---|---|---|
| Ajaokuta | Kogi | DN51 | | Ajaokuta Airstrip |
| Azare | Bauchi | | | Azare Airstrip |
| Bacita | Kwara | | | Bacita Airstrip |

| Bajoga | Gombe | DN54 | | Bajoga Northeast Airport |
|---|---|---|---|---|
| Bebi | Cross River | | | Bebi Airstrip |
| Bida | Niger | DNBI | | Bida Airstrip |
| Eket | Akwa Ibom | DNEK/ DN55 | | Eket Airstrip |
| Escravos | Delta | DN56 | | Escravos Airstrip |
| Gusau | Zamfara | DNGU | QUS | Gusau Airstrip |
| Nguru | Yobe | | | Nguru Airstrip |
| Potiskum | Yobe | | | Potiskum Airstrip |
| Shiroro | Niger | DN50 | | Shiroro Airstrip |
| Tuga | Kebbi | | | Tuga Airstrip |
| **Military Airports** | | | | |
| Katsina | Katsina | DN57 | | Katsina Air Force Base |
| Makurdi | Benue | DNMK | MDI | Makurdi Air Force Base |
| Port Harcourt | Rivers | | PHG | Port Harcourt NAF Base |
| Kaduna | Kaduna | DN53 | | Kaduna Air Force Base |

Sources:

*International Airports. Federal Airports Authority of Nigeria (FAAN). Archived from the original on 24 January 2015. Retrieved 23 April 2010. Major domestic airports. Federal Airports Authority of Nigeria (FAAN). Archived from the original on 26 January 2015. Retrieved 23 April 2010. Other domestic airports. Federal Airports Authority of Nigeria (FAAN). Archived from the original on 26 January 2015. Retrieved 23 April 2010.*

# 5. CHALLENGES OF NIGERIA AVIATION INDUSTRY

Despite the flourishing advances in Nigeria's aviation industry, like a growing child with his or her teething problems, the industry has equally struggled through several stages of development and growth.

These issues have negatively impacted on operations and management of the industry and when you look at any industry, operations and management can be likened to the backbone and blood in a human being. Operational and management problems will always drag an industry back no matter how hard it tries to run ahead. These hiccups though not peculiar to Nigeria, include the skyrocketing of aviation fuel, volatile exchange rate regime and currency devaluations, weak economic regulation of the airlines, dwindling fortune of domestic airlines, high interest rates on funding, frequent interferences on oversight functions and autonomy of NCAA, poor domestic airline consolidation, lack of cooperation and / or merger, lack of coherent air transport policies, dilapidated facilities, poor management and maintenance culture, recurrent air crashes, high and discriminatory insurance premium, insecurity and poor country risk factor, non-discerning of innovative ideals, aging workforce, inadequate air-traffic equipment and controllers, absence of standard training schools for aviation fire fighters and commercial trainees, inadequate hanger maintenance, huge airline indebtedness, etc. There is no success without challenges, and these issues demand a new way of doing things in order to achieve a different and more positive result. Hence, Andrew and Paul, (2015) in their rendition acquiesced that, these issues cause us to think and ask uncomfortable questions, and when we find answers, our industry becomes the better for it.

# CHAPTER TWO

# AVIATION RISK MANAGEMENT: WHERE ARE WE?

Nature is a mother but could be unfriendly in some instances to aviation, in a way we often refer to as "Act of God." This "Act of God" could be predictable. The issue is that humans sometimes don't listen even with bold hand-written warnings, all in the name of making more money and cutting corners. Therefore, underestimating the importance of risk management procedures and practices in the business of aviation has been a major problem for the Nigerian aviation sector.

The aviation sector has, no doubt, proven to be one of the viable pathways to economic progress, growth, and development for many national economies around the globe. This is because the successes of tourism, innovation, import and export, commerce, diplomatic relations, amongst other economic and political endeavours that are transacted across national, trans-national and global jurisdictions are borne upon the wings of a thriving aviation industry.

Imagine the operations of multinationals in Europe, Asia and the US without the speed and comfort provided by the aviation industry. Quite unimaginable, isn't it?

It is estimated that commercial airliners worldwide transport more than four billion passengers and 200 billion tonne-kilometres of cargo annually. However, this is not without risk. Like a medical doctor once said to me as our conversation progressed, "Drinking water comes with risks." In my ignorance, I did ask, "How?" His reply was simple but unexpected "You are not *sure* if you will pass it out or if it goes into your trachea." "Wow!..." was my reply. This was an out-of-classroom insight. The meaning of risk becomes meaningful with reference to probability, likelihood, fear, and exposure to danger. Thus, risk is an integral part of human life.

Fortunately, risk is manageable, even though human thinking, attitude and behaviours towards risk management could compromise lives and properties. Risk and its associated factors could trigger dire consequences for global aviation, and these risks can result from either *uncertainty / beyond-control occurrences*, or *moral hazards*. Therefore, the importance of risk management and its procedures and practices in aviation cannot be overemphasized, especially when we look at the dynamic realities of modern economic development and the fact that several civil aviation disasters have been consequences of failure to follow through on all procedures and / or poor customer service and negligence.

Cutting corners in any area of this pivotally crucial responsibility comes with ripple-effects and the consequences are far reaching. The realities are self-evident: for instance, within our clime, the Zainab Aliyu episode and the Umar Faoruk Abdul-Mutallab episode are examples of cutting-corner activities which would have been fatal were they not promptly and properly managed. I have come to cherish experience as not just a push and pull phenomenon of life, but my teacher as I walked and worked within the Nigerian aviation sector, especially in the area of risk management.

There is definitely an angle in aviation that is purely business and there is another that is simply about humanity. And those who operate within the aviation industry must always bear the latter in mind. Julius Nyerere often referred to 'Ujaama' (you are because we are).

I recall with deep reflection the pictures and faces of family members we visited to deliver messages, not of hope, but of death. The human emotions, the stammering, the expectations coupled with the loss of colleagues, customers, and owners' investments. These scarring memories show that failure spreads like an epidemic, killing people and things. This also tells me that risk involves interactions between three key stakeholders: the *airlines* which provide the fleet of aircraft; the airport authority and *civil aviation authorities* (CAA) which provide and manage the airport, and regulate the operations and practices of the airlines respectively to comply with safety and security best practices both on ground and within the airspace controlled by the aviation authority; and the *customers* who patronize the services of the airlines based on their personal preferences and the quality of services rendered by the airlines.

On whose shoulder would one specifically place certain responsibilities that are mostly pushed around whenever there are issues in aviation? Nostalgically, experience has equipped me with the knowledge that the duty of ensuring safety and security for aircrafts is the responsibility of the airlines and the technical teams; the safety and security of airports and airspaces is the responsibility of the civil aviation authorities; and the safety and security of customers rests on the shoulders of the aforementioned. I will liken these industry players as a whole to a chain reaction, and each of the stakeholders is a link in the chain. For women who adorn themselves with neck chains, how can they use the jewelry if it has broken in one or two places? A weak link in the chain can spell doom for the whole sector.

Risks permeate every human endeavor and to ignore any warning sign is just to be callous. When in some instances, the technical teams are rushed into inspection without documentation and such anomaly is reported, it is organic for the managers to act decisively. But, when at that point the managers use their power to override the position of the technical team, the outcome is quite predictable. On the aspect of reputational risk, we have trampled on people's personal engagements and honour such that those with the means are opting for private jets. When flights are cancelled without human feelings and there are consistent delayed flights without considering that not every passenger on board is embarking on pleasure trip, it is a reminder that the airlines have little or no regard for their customers' interests.

Nigerians have observed the *big-man-nity* philosophy that has affected the security check points and how the *have-nots* are treated without any care or regard. The irony is that a tiny spark is the mother of a mighty fire. Based on my personal experiences and insights from industry professionals, it is the nature and systematic interactions between the key stakeholders that make aviation the most secure and safest means of transportation and travel worldwide. I am talking about synergy and complementary relationships.

The International Air Transport Association (IATA) announced the publication of the 2020 Safety Report and released data for the 2020 safety performance of the commercial airline industry. The total number of accidents decreased from 52 in 2019 to 38 in 2020. The total number of fatal accidents decreased from 8 in 2019 to 5 in 2020. The all-accidents rate was 1.71 accidents per million flights. This is higher than the 5 year (2016-2020) average rate which is 1.38 accidents per million flights. IATA member airlines' accident rate was 0.83 per million flights which was an improvement over the 5-year average rate of 0.96. Total flight operations reduced by 53% to

22 million in 2020. Fatality risk remained unchanged compared to the five-year average at 0.13.

With a fatality risk of 0.13 for air travel, on average, a person would have to travel by air every day for 461 years before experiencing accident with at least one fatality. On average, a person would have to travel every day for 20,932 years to experience a 100% fatal accident. "Flying is safe, although the industry did take a step back in performance in 2020" said Alexandre de Juniac, IATA's director general and CEO. "For the first time in more than 15 years there were no 'Loss of Control In-Flight (LOC-I)' accidents, which have accounted for the largest share of fatalities since 2016", he said. Pilots whose pay is in arrears of 6 months or who cut corners in medicals or get drunk few hours to the flight, will be mentally unstable and will sure lose control in flight.

Meanwhile, any fatal air accident brings sad news to families. This brings to mind the assumption that, indeed, and as many experts would agree, in the business of aviation, fatal accidents do not occur without cause; but are, mostly typically, the products of systemic failures caused by negligence, carelessness and the readiness to cut corners in a bid to save costs at the expense of safety.

"Ambition is sweetly blind. As it propels the mind to productive energy, so does it hide a multitude of faults and grave consequences," says Adeeyo (2018). This statement rightly captures the incident that happened on October 29, 2018. The news of the illfated flight JT610 involving a Boeing Jet operated by Lion Air, an Indonesian airline company made global headlines. The domestic passenger flight was enroute Pangkal Pinang on the tin-mining island of Bangka from Jakarta, the country's capital, but lost contact with the control tower 13 minutes after take-off, with flight data showing that the aircraft had taken a sudden sharp dive into the Java Sea just few minutes after the 31-year-old Indian pilot, Captain Bhavye Suneja, had requested clearance and received approval to return the aircraft to take-off base at the Soekarno Hatta International Airport, possibly after noticing unmanageable faults. One hundred and eighty-nine people perished in the crash which industry experts have referred to as arguably the "country's second worst air disaster since 1997".

The ill-fated aircraft was a Boeing 737 Max 8 Jet. As at the time of the crash, the aircraft was of the latest Boeing model that was only launched globally by the American aircraft manufacturer the previous year as an improvement in fuel efficiency compared to the common 737 jets range, and is reported to have been in use for less than three months before the day of the crash. In addition, the new aircraft included "...an automated system that pushes the nose down if a sensor detects it is pointed so high [that] the plane is at risk of an aerodynamic stall."[1] However, media reports by the airline's chief executive, Edward Sirait, confirmed that the very aircraft had showed signs of a serious technical fault the previous night on a flight presumably from Bali to Jakarta, but had still been cleared by engineers as fit to fly only a few hours later (the next day). This was corroborated by Nurcahyo Utomo, the head of Indonesia's National Transport Safety Committee (KNKT).

As expected, the families and relations of the victims of the ill-fated flight asked questions and demanded answers, and a forensic investigation was launched to uncover the realities surrounding the crash. The Australian Government instructed its officials not to fly Lion Air until investigations into the crash had yielded conclusive results. A few weeks later, investigation reports revealed that the aircraft was not airworthy following recurrent technical issues since a flight that it embarked on the day before the crash, in which the pilot had to shut down the plane's anti-stall system to be able to make it safely to Jakarta. According to a statement made by Nurcahyo Utomo to newsmen, "…the plane was no longer airworthy and should not have continued flying." The investigation report further discovered critical vulnerabilities and inconsistencies in the safety culture of Lion Air, and how aircraft repairs are documented, with one media source reporting that "Lion Air kept putting the plane back into service despite repeatedly failing to fix a problem with the airspeed indicator [angle of attack (AOA) sensors] in the [up to four] days leading up to the fatal flight," which elevates concerns about "problems with key systems in one of the world's newest and most advanced commercial passenger planes."[2] Interestingly, the privately-owned parent company *Lion Air Group* which hosts the airline and also operates Batik Air and Wings Air is said to have captured half of the domestic air travel market in Southeast Asia in less than 20 years of operations, despite a growing reputation of "dubious safety records and an avalanche of complaints over shoddy service." *Ibid* A few of the many questions that yet linger in many minds are: "If the ill-fated aircraft was meant to have been declared as not airworthy since many days before the fatal flight, how then was it still flying commercially?" "Could the crash have been a result of cutting corners (perhaps, in a bid to minimize costs and optimize profit) in the areas of adequate maintenance and safety risk management on the part of the airline?" Well, maybe.

## THE AIRCRAFT: PARTS, OPERATIONS AND RISKS

Safety remains one of the principal and most critical challenges that modern aviation businesses have to grapple with. One thing that is obvious is that unlike other means of transportation, there are no terminals, stations or stop-points in the air. In such instances, a problem of a few seconds could result in heavy casualties hence safety becomes non-negotiable since aircrafts cannot park mid-air to have critical faults fixed whenever they occur during commuting. The grain of the challenge therefore lies in maintaining commercial aircrafts in such a pristine and optimum operating condition and to do everything that will ensure that qualified personnel fix visible or detectable faults before it is too late.

Simply stated, risk management refers to the procedures and practices that are applied to ensure the safety of commercial payloads: man (passengers), goods (cargo) and machine (the aircraft) throughout the period(s) of commuting. Like my analogy of the industry as a chain with the stakeholders as links in it, circumspect risk management in this information technology age requires a coordination of all applicable contingencies of people, processes, procedures, structures and resources, which must be taken into consideration in trying to identify possible hazards, understand risks, envisage implications, and deploy effective management and control measures to mitigate the impact of incidents in the event of disaster. Thus, modern aircrafts can be generally divided into four essential parts: the engines, the fuselage, the auxiliary power unit (APU), landing gears and appendages. If risk management practices are to be efficient, there are mandatory checks that the aircraft operators are required to adhere to in order to maintain all these parts in the best operating conditions throughout the entire span of usage of the aircraft.

The aircraft is a complex and technically crafted machine that must be appreciated and handled with utmost maintenance and care. The propulsion system of a regular aircraft has an engine unit that includes one or more engines, which are typically either piston engines or gas turbines that generate the mechanical power (assisted by a propeller/propulsion pump), needed to thrust the aircraft through the air at very high speeds. The fuselage of the aircraft essentially refers to the main body of the aircraft which includes the cockpit, cabin and aisle of the passenger seating section, and cargo holding section. The fuselage serves to position the aircraft for control and stability, which makes it maneuverable as it is being lifted through the air (aided by the wings).

The auxiliary power unit (APU) usually located on the tail section of the plane is a rather noisy component that serves as the power generating system of the aircraft. By generally producing up to 115V of alternating current (AC) at 400 Hz, or 28V of direct current (DC), the APU generates the supplementary electrical power needed to provide ignition to the main engine; light the fuselage and provide air conditioning for a conducive flight environment; and power flight systems, cockpit avionics, as well as hydraulics when the aircraft is at rest or experiencing a flight emergency. Appendages play other crucial roles in supporting an aircraft as it navigates through air and on arrival on the ground – the rudder, spoilers, stabilizers, winglet, elevator, landing gear and wheel system, amongst others.

The goal of the propulsion system (which is usually housed in the wings or tail/stabilizer of the bird-shaped passenger aircraft, with exception to helicopters) is basically to generate enough aerodynamic thrust force to balance out the drag force that is imposed by the fuselage with its compositions and appendages while the aircraft is cruising; which thrust force must then sufficiently exceed the drag force in order for the aircraft to accelerate. In other words, the greater the excess thrust force (i.e., the positive difference between the thrust and drag forces), the greater the speed of acceleration of the aircraft.

It is greed and gross irresponsibility that pushes one to regard the aircraft as a mere transportation machine. From the brief description of the major components of an aircraft, we can see that the modern aircraft is a complex integrated system of various components, each having its specific function(s) but no less indispensable to the efficient functioning of the airplane. In many cases, aviation incidents and accidents are usually the result of the multiplier ripple effects of a convolution of various risk factors falling apart across the full spectrum of the safe operational standards and safety structures of the aircraft, as well as the safety and security frameworks of airlines.

## PROFILING RISKS TO AVIATION SAFETY

Understanding risk as a generic term may give rise to a situation whereby some minute but salient issues may be overlooked in aviation risk discussions. Therefore, I want us to conceptualize a risk as an event that could result in a compromise of safety. Risks to aviation safety can be broadly classified either as risks due to uncertainty, or risks due to hazards.

a. ***Uncertainty risks/beyond-control occurrences*** *are generally risks which are quite and to a large extent beyond the control of the airlines. They usually emanate from factors that relate to natural causes such as wind shears, microbursts, volcanoes and volcanic ash, bird strikes, desert and forest fires/smoke/fog, weather, quakes and tsunamis, amongst other natural causes.*

b. ***Hazard risks***, *on the other hand, are risks that are often originated and propagated by human, technological and other non-natural causes. They are often the result of personnel shortcomings, unattended physical faults or ergonomic defects, system/equipment malfunction and failure, dangerous elements (weaponry, animals, toxic plants, and chemicals) and violence, amongst others.*

Fortunately, modern advancements in science and technology have made it possible for uncertainty risks to be predictable and detected to a remarkable degree of precision and accuracy (e.g., frost/snow/ice, clouds, rain storms, wind and hurricanes, heavy strikes from lightning and thunder, quakes/tsunamis, etc.), so that airliners can be informed about the imminence of uncertainty risks well ahead of time to enable them apply caution in order to avert disaster.

Let me also state that the onus of ensuring safety and security against risks that could emanate from hazards remain the responsibility of the airlines/airline operators. I have mentioned earlier the possibility of human beings ignoring warnings for the sake of gain. It is therefore important for aviation businesses to consistently maintain optimum safety and maintain best practices in order to minimize and possibly eliminate risks that could result from hazards.

In the table on Risk Profile of Aviation Safety Hazards below, profiles of some of the most common risk factors to aviation safety that have been known to result in hazards capable of leading to disaster under critical conditions are presented. Quite a number of human hazards can be prevented by frequent trainings, education and medical checks, as well as structural/ functions redesigns of certain parts of the aircraft to provide support for disability.

Quite a number of system hazards can be prevented by routine maintenance, inspection and pre-flight testing; in the same vein, physical hazards can be mitigated by frequent checks, quality assessments, and robust insurance policies to reduce financial liabilities in the event of an incident; while thorough pre-flight screening, cargo checks, and inspection procedures would help mitigate hazards that could result from other hazardous causes. Runways are very crucial to airline operation. Runway hazards though minor compared to mid- air hazard, could be fatal.

Hazards could be minimized, if not completely prevented, by strict adherence to routine airport maintenance schedules as well as collaborative and corroborative pre-flight runway inspections by ground (security) personnel and flight officials. While hazards that could result from violence can best be mitigated by maintaining security best practices and procedures including thorough pre- flight security screening, as well as good diplomatic relations between countries, especially in times of conflict.

## TABLE 1: RISK PROFILE OF AVIATION SAFETY HAZARDS

| S/N | Safety Risk Factors | | Description | Hazards |
|---|---|---|---|---|
| | *Superclass* | *Subclass* | | |
| 1. | | | | |
| | Physiology | Pilot Fatigue/ Intoxication | Tiring out of the pilot as a result of having flown an aircraft for long hours and frequent violations of rest time, OR poor coordination by the pilot due to intoxication from alcohol or other substances. | Human Hazards |
| | | Misinterpretation | Misunderstanding critical information whether relating to flight status, aircraft operations, environmental conditions, crew management, etc. | |

| | | Sudden Health Incident | The sudden onset and aggravation of an unforeseen health incident on cabin and crew members during flight. Generally, resulting from expired medicals. | |
|---|---|---|---|---|
| | | Human Error | Unwitting mistakes by flight officials, passengers, or cabin crew during flight; or by ground personnel before / after flight. e.g., a pilot unknowingly stalling an aircraft; a passenger leaving a hand luggage lying loosely around during flight; a cabin crew not docking a trolley after use; a heavy repairs equipment left behind by an engineer or maintenance office; an engineer misconfiguring. | |
| | | Disability | Disabled individuals aboard aircrafts that do not have adequate utilities to support their disabilities could be at risk of grievous bodily injury that could result in death to themselves or other individuals on board. | |
| 2. | | Misinformation Malfunction | Flight systems generating wrong information about flight status, aircraft operations, | System Hazards |

| | | | | |
|---|---|---|---|---|
| | | | environmental conditions, crew management, etc., due to faulty sensors, (electromagnetic) interference, poor calibration, or reading mechanisms. | |
| 3. | | Non-information | Flight systems failing to provide / transmit necessary information at critical times (possibly due to successful or ongoing hacks/breaches). | |
| | Failure | Damage | Flight systems/ mechanisms suddenly going bad due to progressively unnoticed defects; mechanical wears/fatigue; or as a result of impact caused by foreign objects / debris during flights | |
| | | Energy Insufficiencies | Failure could also result from energy insufficiencies/ mishaps such as fuel starvation, electrical surges, short-circuiting and overheating, power drains, etc. | |
| 4. | Other | Animals Causes | Dangerous/deadly animals (reptiles, amphibians, or mammals) appearing on board an aircraft during flight. | Dangerous Elements |

| | | Weaponry | Lethal weapons/explosives poorly packed and stored on board the aeroplane | |
|---|---|---|---|---|
| 5. | | Chemicals | Dangerous / inflammable chemicals poorly packed and stored on board the aeroplane. | |
| | | Toxic Plants | Plant species that are injurious or toxic to breathing, sensing and coordination, which are poorly packed and stored on board the plane. | |
| | Physical | Environment | These are hazards that could result from physical faults and defects in the cabin environment, such as uneven stairs, noisy cabins and engines, low hanging ceilings, naked wires dangling out. | |
| 6. | | Ergonomic | These are hazards that could result from cabin utilities that have deteriorated in quality, such as loose seats and weak seat frames, torn seatbelts, ripped/sunken upholstery, broken armrests, etc. | |
| | Runway | Bad runways | Bad runways that are uneven, riddled with potholes, poorly lighted or unmarked could pose | Ground Hazards |

| | | | hazards to aircrafts during take-off / landing. | |
|---|---|---|---|---|
| | | Livestock And Equipment | Livestock and heavy equipment that are not cleared off from the runway urgently could pose ground hazards to aircraft. | |
| 7. | | War | Aircrafts that wander into airspaces of countries that are at war face the risk of being shot down. | |
| | Violence and Violent Attacks | Terrorism | Subversive control of the aircraft by terrorists or other malicious entities, which could possibly result in the aircraft being forced to navigate / cruise into unsafe and dangerous terrains. | Third- party Hazards |

Each and every aircraft incident/accident investigation bureau reports continue to confirm that failure to adhere to strict safety routines and precautions could easily and very quickly spiral out of control and result in disaster, injury and death. Cutting costs in any area of aviation safety that predisposes an aircraft to any of these above hazards basically translates to Cutting Corners. Any professional misconduct, and/or ethical failure, which present an ominous danger sign for the safety of the aircraft, passengers, cargo and crew, will be tantamount to cutting corners.

## WHERE ARE WE?

The International Civil Aviation Organization (ICAO) and the International Air Transport Association (IATA), two bodies that act as our industry watchdogs, have laid out minimum standards and recommended practices (SARPs) that must be carefully followed to keep all essential parts of the aircraft in their best shape, and to ensure an all-round degree of safety for the aircraft and everything it carries (man, cargo, and the machine itself). ICAO defines *standards* as "any specification for physical characteristics, configuration, material, performance, personnel or procedure, the uniform application of which is recognized as necessary for the safety or regularity of international air navigation and to which Contracting States will conform in accordance with the Convention;" while *recommended practices* are "any specification for physical characteristics, configuration, material, performance, personnel or procedure, the uniform application of which is recognized as desirable in the interest of safety, regularity or efficiency of international air navigation and to which Contracting States will endeavour to conform in accordance with the Convention"[3].These standards and recommended practices are dynamic, in response to technological advances, research, insight from accident investigations, and other necessities.

For a global industry like ours' ICAO SARPs are intended to "assist States in managing aviation safety risks, in coordination with their Service Providers,"[4] and is able to verify compliance with the SARPs through periodic audits of documentary evidence kept by state oversight systems and agencies (usually under the jurisdiction of national CAAs) under its Universal Safety Oversight Audit Programme (USOAP), and Universal Security Audit Programme (USAP). Airlines are then required to comply with these minimum standards and recommended practices, as enforced by national CAAs, or higher standards in the operation of their fleet, either according to a periodic schedule (routines) or based on utilization (flight hours covered). Any of the CAAs that fails or falls short of the requirements would face the risk of being blacklisted by ICAO for failing in the responsibility of enforcing compliance to the SARPs within their jurisdictions.

While the approach of ICAO is aimed at holding CAAs responsible for the compliance of all airlines operated in their jurisdiction with universal SARPs, IATA, on the other hand, being a trade association of 290 major carrier airlines representing 117 countries is focused on holding the airlines themselves responsible for compliance with universal SARPs. IATA member airlines in addition to ICAO / SARPSs, raised the standard through its Operational Safety Audit (IOSA). As I have said earlier, these safety audits are being reviewed from time to time and expanded by many conventions and annexes, and they are published in various publicly available industry documents. The SARPs specified by ICAO include: safety operations for the cabin[5]; managing fatigue; safety initiatives and management; training and reporting; medical standards; policy recommendations relating to the possession and use of portable transportation devices, portable electronic devices, and electronic cigarettes; handling carry-on baggage and pets in the cabin; emotional support animals like seeing-eye dogs that help the bind to navigate; specifications for general safety management and training strategies; recommendations for aircraft owners and operators covering all phases of the aircraft end-of-life process; guidelines for improving safety; efficiency and operational integrity of aircrafts; specifications for project management and risks involved in cabin layout, retrofit and entry into service [678910] amongst scores of other SARPs documentations.

It is quite unfortunate that corruption and nepotism have so far crippled promising economies like Nigeria, and have been able to creep into a strategic sector like aviation, sometimes effectively truncating the very mandates and purposes for which safety risk management & standard and recommended practices (SARPs) were established. I have seen this happen through falsified documentations, bribery and intimidation of regulatory inspectors, administrative oppression and bullying of pilots, engineers, as well as airline safety and quality control personnel, all in a bid to cut costs.

The chain of Nigeria's airline industry is consistently endangered by weak-links, as aviators continue to cut corners every now and then.

## RESPONSIBLE RISK MANAGEMENT WITHOUT CUTTING CORNERS

One big question then comes to mind: must operating at a purse-friendly cost (which remains a cardinal goal of business engagements) always be done at the expense of safety in aviation business? Are there no other ways of cutting costs without cutting corners and compromising safety in aviation?

One of the biggest challenges to aircraft routine maintenance as part of aviation risk management, emanates from the fact that in many instances, all four essential parts (propulsion system, fuselage, APU, gears and appendages) of the aircrafts in a fleet operated by an airline may come together from entirely different manufacturers to make up a single aircraft and with each manufacturer sometimes laying out a set of safety and maintenance procedures/routines that could differ largely one from another. Let me postulate a hypothetical example. An aircraft designed by Boeing could be fitted with a Rolls Royce engine; another aircraft designed by Airbus could be powered by an engine manufactured by Pratt and Whitney; while yet another aircraft designed by Embraer could be powered by an engine produced by General Electric. Each manufacturer could have its own Airplane Maintenance Manual (AMM) that outlines safety procedures and recommends maintenance routines to airlines who operate such aircrafts in their fleet. In some instances, all three different aircrafts could be part of the fleet operated by a single airline in a particular country.

In my opinion, when it comes to cutting costs in the aviation business, one of the most financially prudent and business-savvy path for airliners/airline operators is to operate a common fleet of aircrafts with common parts either from the same manufacturer/ leasor or from extensively similar manufacturer product lines. This would ensure that safety and maintenance routines are viewed less by the aviators in terms of the huge costs that would be required to hire entirely different teams of different fleet engineers to service the various parts of all aircrafts in the fleet; but instead, the same team of specialist engineers can be hired to service and maintain the entire fleet of aircrafts for much lower costs as all parts are either the same or extensively similar. The disadvantage of single fleet however, is the grounding of the entire common fleet in the event of an accident when other fleet type could have sustained flight operations while investigations are ongoing. Remember, the word "Accident" is defined as an event happening with cause/s unknown.

One other consideration for cutting costs is by minimizing the sector fuel consumption of the aircraft so as to cut down on the associated financial implication. In view of the progress in aviation technology, two ways to achieve this are to:

1. Optimize the load factor (lift-to-weight ratio) of the aircraft

2. Opt for clean and renewable energy alternatives and supplement for jet propulsion (such as the now commercially available fully-electric, turboelectric and hybrid-electric jet propulsion systems) as opposed to the high-cost and environmental consequences associated with total reliance on fossilized energy.

This consideration is based on the fact that: (a) An optimized load factor would contribute to a lower drag force generated by the fuselage, which would be easier to balance out by the propulsion system of the airplane; and (b) Jet propulsion systems that rely on clean and renewable energy sources are much less expensive energy alternatives to traditional propulsion systems that operate on rapid fuel consumption to power the pistons and turbines of the engine(s) in order to generate sufficient force that will thrust the aircraft through the air. Therefore, by limiting the amount of work that the propulsion system would have to do, and using energy sources that are clean, renewable, and readily available, airliners can conserve expensive fueling costs.

One practical example of a way to reduce the load factor of the fuselage on commercial civil airliners that commute domestically is to store out safety gear, lifejackets that might not be necessary if the airliner would not have to fly over water. An average Type I Portable Flotation Devices (PFDs) / lifejacket with a minimum buoyancy rating of 22 pounds could weigh up to one pound. The cumulative weight resulting from this on a commercial passenger aircraft with a multiclass seating configuration can be up to 500 pounds (*227*). This gives a picture of the resulting energy and cost savings that could come from doing away with such weight on an aircraft. Another way is to regulate the body weight of the cabin crew members to a set limit. newspapers, magazines, journals, etc in electronic form are significant cost cutting measures on weight limitations.

The resulting cost savings could then be ploughed-back into more frequent maintenance and safety inspection schedules, more robust technical trainings, and better qualified personnel, which could all help to bring about better risk management.

In addition, civil aviation authorities can get more value for money by establishing and adhering to strict routines for safety inspections, maintenance routines, and regulatory/policy specifications regarding corporate governance, quality control, fleet management, amongst other key areas of the aviation business. This is because routine operations would always be cumulatively more cost-effective in the longer term than sudden comprehensive schedules, especially in areas of safety and maintenance. More often than not, airlines do cut corners when monthly maintenance reserves are not set aside but consumed in operations. When the CAA fails to deliver on its responsibility of providing and managing a safe and risk-free airport and airspace, the ripple effects of the results are indeed threatening. Airports and airspaces can also be closed down for maintenance during peak seasons which can be a big blow for licensed operators. An entire fleet could be retired as unsafe and not airworthy due to quality shortcomings that have become irreparable and cannot be ameliorated due to prolonged degradation.

# CHAPTER THREE

# TRAVEL AGENT AND TRAVEL MANAGEMENT COMPANY (TMC) - MOLUE (Mass Transit Bus) MENTALITY

*Good customer service for flights begins with the travel agent and or travel management companies (TMCs). If the beginning is not right, the strongest links further down the line could be very devastating and disastrous.*

A journalist once asked me, "what is the difference and or similarities between travel agents and travel management companies?" Interesting question that shuddered me a bit but I was up to the task as my years of experience in the aviation industry were not about to fail me. Travel agencies and travel management companies are bridges between expanse of waters separating the customers and service providers. Service providers in this case are the airlines, hotels, rent a car companies, restaurants, cruise lines, and tour operators. Contract of carriage / hospitality is established between the two by the travel agent.

TMCs beyond the contract of carriage/hospitality, go to meet corporate regulators and set limits on travel finance such as class of travel, limit of tariff costs, allowances and general travel expenses by corporate organization travelers. While the travel agent deals with occasional leisure travel needs, a travel management company provides on-going services with the objective of providing cost savings, keeping control of a travel policy and allowing the client to spend less time on time-consuming travel arrangements.

The success and sustenance of any business depends largely on a satisfied customer base and it is no different with the aviation business. Travel agencies will have to sell the right locations and trips to the right person(s) in the most efficient and cost-effective way possible. Indeed, travel agencies play a major role in the smooth running of the aviation industry. By this I mean that the travel agencies are often the first point of contact for aviation customers. They are travel experts and consultants who could be likened to gatekeepers of the industry.

Efficient travel agency management goes a long way in keeping customers satisfied and willing to do business again with the several players in the aviation value chain.

Selling individually customised trips could be complex, considering the peculiar needs of customers, so it requires an increased level of automation. The avenue for interaction between the travel agencies and customers presented by information technology makes automation easy and user-friendly, even though not without challenges. Moreover, identification and implementation of stateof-the-art software solutions as well as properly engineered processes is therefore essential for successful travel agency management.

Travel agencies all over the world are accredited by the International Air Transport Association (IATA). IATA ensures strict adherence to travel agency management standards and consequently sets the tone for customer satisfaction. As I have earlier stated, travel agencies hold so much together for the smooth running of the entire industry value chain as they are involved in airline seat reservations, taxi and train boarding, hotel reservations, and overall impact on the travel and tourism income in any country.

Proper management of agents who are the providers of these services is very essential especially in a country like Nigeria where less than five percent of the available aviation wealth has so far been explored.

Travel agencies represent the downstream distribution sector of airlines and travel trade and is the sector with the closest interaction with the customers, hence they are likened to gatekeepers. A properly run travel agency is therefore essential for ensuring repeat business, and IATA accreditation represents a major step for ensuring effective and efficient travel agency management.

IATA accreditations do not come easy because travel agencies need to show competencies in the quality of operations, quality of staff, services and capital base. This sometimes discourages interested investors, driving some into operating agencies that are not accredited. In Nigeria for instance, most of the travel agencies are not IATA accredited and are contributors to the poor state of aviation business in Nigeria. Operational efficiency of travel agencies relies on the use of state-of-the-art travel agency distribution software among other automated and well-engineered processes. IATA accredited agencies have access to these technologies through the involvement of Global Distribution Systems (GDS)s. GDSs provide a marketplace for all the players in the aviation industry: airlines, hotels, road transportation companies, shipping companies, travel agents and customers. GDSs through IATA Billing Settlement Plans (BSP) and various back office solutions, enable seamless billing and payment systems across the aviation market as well as other automated products to make the entire aviation experience a memorable one.

I find it rather disturbing that despite IATA accreditation of agencies to enhance efficiency and deployment of GDS offerings, the Nigeria aviation industry has not lived up to its full potential.

In a bid to reduce costs, some African airlines especially in Nigeria try to bypass the GDSs which will strategically position their inventory globally beyond Nigerian borders and avail market opportunities outside their website reach.

Indeed, in my opinion, the Nigeria travel agency management breathes life into the age-long saying: "Penny wise, pound foolish". It can be said that failure to take advantage of available state-of-theart technological solutions in any endeavour is an invitation to inefficiency and poor use of resources, which will eventually bleed any business to death. In the aviation industry which avails one of the most direct links to the rest of the world (via the airspace), this folly becomes even more obvious and visible.

As far as I am concerned, the chief purpose of establishing a business is to make profit and any business owner worth his salt is primarily concerned with the reduction of operational costs while increasing profit margins. The aviation industry requires a certain level of investment for sustainable growth. These issues came up when the aviation correspondent of The PUNCH newspaper interviewed me in 2017. In my appraisal, I told him when growth is not sustained, there can never be development. Regrettably, the sector cannot be said to be developed since growth of all the value chain is abysmally low and not sustained.

Growth of travel agencies have improved significantly as evidenced by increased number of IATA accredited agencies while the dearth in this regard is evidenced in the ever-increasing ratio of unaccredited agencies. The high number of travel agencies operating below acceptable global standards can be traced to the poor development of the industry in Nigeria.

What then can be done to encourage travel agencies to make necessary investments for IATA accreditation, seeing that they form a major part of the aviation ecosystem and the Nigerian Corporate Affairs Commission (CAC) does not require that travel agencies be IATA certified before being incorporated? It makes common sense to conclude that, most incorporated travel agencies may not be qualified given professional demands.

As I have stated earlier, the major concern of any business owner is profit making, therefore any encouragement for the adoption of best practices must be followed with corresponding plan to increase profit. The first pointer of the promising financial prospects through IATA certification is the sheer influence the body has in the aviation industry. About 265 global airline relationships are handled by IATA, translating to 83 percent of the international air traffic by IATA airlines. Tapping into such a vast network of operators would definitely go a long way in improving the bottom line of travel agencies.

When you look at it from the perspective of a wise investor, access to approximately 250 IATA airline members through a single standard sales agency agreement is the stuff of dreams for savvy travel agency owners interested in making profits without compromising on quality. With the certification, travel agencies get the authorization to sell international and/or local tickets on behalf of the airlines. The opportunity to work with IATAs billing settlement plan (BSP) should be major bait for discerning travel agency/ travel management companies. Access to the BSP and BSP Link for the provision of a single standard interface for invoicing and payments between travel agents, airlines and multiple travel trade providers, is not something to be overlooked by seriousminded, profit-seeking travel agency companies.

I can succinctly submit here with every form of authority that the global appeal attained by affiliating with IATA cannot be over emphasized. IATA provides a unique identifier for travel agents via a numeric code ensuring global travel industry recognition in the process. IATA accredited travel agents enjoy an enhanced visibility which consequently enhances the confidence of global consumers especially at the sight of the IATA logo and branding displayed at the travel agency office and /or website. Knowing that an agency is certified eases customers' nerves and increases the possibility of repeat business. Are you, like me, wondering why some travel agents are not trying their best to do what it takes to be able to exploit these advantages? You can make an informed conclusion and find the answers to your questions.

# CHAPTER FOUR

## CORPORATE GOVERNANCE:
### The Missing Link

There is this popular saying in some African cultures: "A broom stick is easily broken, but the bunch has the strength." It has been well stated that unity is strength and in business, there will always be unity whenever stakeholders' interests are harnessed. This is the call for corporate governance. According to writers Mbu- Ogar, Effiong and Abang, in their work on corporate governance published in 2017, corporate governance is a single body of structures, systems, mechanisms and framework through which organizations are directed and controlled by those saddled with the duties and responsibilities in the interest of shareholders and other stakeholders. The Guardian Newspaper reported Banjo, a former director at the defunct Virgin Nigeria Airlines, on corporate governance as to address measures that are aimed at managing and reducing financial and operational risks by building the integrity, transparency and accountability of a company's board and management.

Having this in mind, one also has to note that global transportation has an inevitable impact on every individual, organization and nation as it remains the basis for social network and interactions on every sphere of life. No matter the preferred or chosen means of transportation, be it road, rail, sea or air, movement is inevitable. The aviation sector is an incentive for the financial / economic growth of countries. It is a wheel that drives financial exercises. It encourages exchange, helps profitability in the economy and improves effectiveness in the flexible chain. It is an empowering agent for ventures and can spike innovation. Fundamentally, it is a wellspring of value business. Consequently, it is a key sector deserving a guarded plot to success if Nigeria desires development. In Nigeria, the aviation industry has come a long way in history and is noted as one of the most important drivers of national growth and development, contributing over NGN58 billion to the GDP of the nation and creating over 61,000 jobs. Since 1925, when the first airplane was said to have landed in Kano, Nigeria, several commercial airlines have been seen to rise and fall shortly after, despite the huge potential in the industry. Casting our memory back in time, airlines like the Okada Air, Kabo, Harco, Harca, ADC, Bellview, EAS, Chanchangi, Sosoliso and Al Barka amongst others have – at some point – served the needs of customers in the commercial aviation sector in Nigeria.

The aviation industry has indeed over the years struggled under the weight of several challenges that have hindered growth and has crippled business possibilities in the sector. These challenges include: lack of reliable and accurate meteorological forecasts before take-off and landing, lack of adequate investments in the training of pilots and engineers that operate the air planes, poor adherence to maintenance schedules and replacement culture, poor management system, corruption, the godfather syndrome, and many more.

I have been pondering on this question for a while: could corporate governance be the missing link responsible for all or most of our challenges? Tighten your seat belt as we take a swift flight into the world of corporate governance in the aviation industry.

In the assessment of former managing director of Virgin Nigeria Airways and currently the CEO of Ropeways, Captain Dapo Olumide (in his interview with THISDAY), one of the reasons why airlines in Nigeria fail is lack of corporate governance. He said "…an airline should have the kind of people in the board that will question decisions taken that are not good for the sustenance of that company". Also, aviation regulatory bodies like the Nigeria Civil Aviation Authority (NCAA) must develop the courage to insist that corporate governance be adhered to thus reducing family relations representation; the lavish lifestyle of airline owners which takes precedence over payment of pilots, engineers and shareholders; staff becoming contractors for services thereby compromising standards; and the chairman of the airline taking decisions to buy an aircraft that runs into several billions of naira without robust business case and due diligence.

A report from the Airline Operators of Nigeria (AON) in 2016 reveals that over forty- seven (47) promising Nigerian indigenous companies representing about 85% of the indigenous airlines have folded up within the last 30 years. The right question to ask is: What could be responsible for such high level of collapse? The major problem, the root of it all, is the lack of good corporate governance that is hinged on four basic pillars (accountability, responsibility, fairness and transparency) by which organizations are supposed to be controlled, directed or piloted to achieve the purpose of their existence which includes, maximizing profit and improving relationships with customers and other stake holders.

According to the International Air Transport Association (IATA), 71% of aviation accidents are due to human error, with other causes being ageing aircrafts with some beyond economic repair (BER), poor weather and deficiencies in safety management systems. IATA whose airline members represent 93% of global air traffic, stated in a report monitored in The Punch, published on the 30th of December 2005, that only three of Africa's 39 IATA members had completed their IATA operational safety audit (IOSA) since 2005 and renewed periodically. The three members are South Africa Airways, Egypt Air and Kenya Airways. It is surprising to note that at that time, no Nigerian airline was IOSA certified despite high accident rate. This should have called for a more sober and focused approach to safety. Things have however improved today. Few Nigerian Airlines are IOSA certified: Air Peace, Arik and Aero. However, most Nigerian airlines are not IATA members or African Airlines Association (AFRAA) members not to talk of IOSA certified.

However, one begins to wonder the strategy behind management of Nigerian commercial airlines. Should it not be targeted at giving quality service, and at the same time protecting the interests of the investors while satisfying the managerial expectations of the board members? In a bid to salvage more companies from failing and still forestall more fatal accidents from occurring, the Federal Government of Nigeria in recent times has carried out some hostile takeovers of some airlines through the Asset Management Corporation of Nigeria (AMCON) with fingers pointing at the inability of the board of directors of the affected firms to keep the companies afloat within acceptable standards by cutting costs without necessarily cutting corners. The companies affected are: Aero Contractors with a new ownership structure of 60:40 between the government and the Ibru family, and Arik Air Limited with a total replacement of the drivers of the company's affairs.

Corporate governance is indeed a missing link in the chain and has brought down several promising airlines.

Oh! How I look forward to an undiluted free and fair appointment of board members without halo-effect and the godfather syndrome playing out. The aviation industry in Nigeria will live up to its full potential if the board of directors run with the principle of "*cutting costs without cutting corners*" by operating on the four basic pillars of corporate governance (accountability, responsibility, fairness and transparency). The issues I have observed as the causes of these challenges and eventual fold up of the once-promising companies are clearly in-house issues that should have been properly handled by the board and management of the respective airlines. I have been able to observe these challenges as they hinder growth and swallow up development opportunities and in the face of these challenges, customers, who are meant to be 'kings' as far as businesses are concerned, become the least in the turn-out of events.

The question then arises, even though the answer is obvious: whose responsibility is it to resolve these issues? One is tempted to say the government should enforce compliance, but it is not the responsibility of government to manage private businesses as dictators or to meddle in every corporate challenge. This should be the sole responsibility of the management and board of directors of the companies. As such, we have to look carefully into the issue of *corporate governance*. What is it, and what is it not?

## CHALLENGES FACING CORPORATE GOVERNANCE IN NIGERIAN AIRLINES

Corporate governance, as defined earlier, embodies structures, systems, mechanisms and frameworks through which organizations are directed and controlled by those saddled with the duties and responsibilities in the interest of shareholders and other industry stakeholders. Authors Robert A.G Monks and Nell Minow, in their book, 'Corporate Governance', describe a company as a mechanism which allows diverse parties to contribute finance, expertise and labour for the utmost benefit of all concerned. Professor Marc Sternberg, a professor of law, and an expert on corporate governance, argues that the purpose of a company is to capitalize on owner's value over a long term through the sale of goods and services. Similarly, Authors Shleifer and Vishny in a journal published in 1997 were of the view that corporate governance is the way that suppliers of finance (investors) receive a return on investment from the managers to whom they have entrusted their funds. Their emphasis was on the agency theory perspective, which expresses the agreement between one party (the principal) who provides finance to another party (the agent) who has been employed to manage a company in the interest of its stakeholders.

The agency theory places emphasis on shareholders' value as the chief objective of an organization.

However, some scholars like Anthony Henry and Edward Freeman diverged from the shareholder view, as they are of the stakeholder proponents. Stakeholder proponents argue that the existence of a company, even with availability of lots of investable funds, depends on the effect of the decisions of the organization on different stakeholders which could be internal or external. They emphasized the importance of management's role in balancing each stakeholders needs, rather than focusing on shareholders only. Therefore, the collapse of some major airlines and companies such as Okada Air, Kabo, Harco, Harca, ADC, Bellview, EAS, Chanchangi, Sosoliso, Al Barka, Ansett Airlines, Harka Airways, amongst others, brought the issue of corporate governance to greater limelight and consciousness.

A major recommendation of past Aviation Safety Roundtable Initiative popularly called (ART) conferences held in Nigeria between 2018 and 2019, has seen a yearning of aviation experts to instill corporate governance culture in the various airline operations in Nigeria and ensure that transparency and accountability are imbibed. An assertion to this was the outcry of AMCON boss, Ahmed Kuru, who pointed out that the germane reason for the failure of about 160 Nigeria airlines, is traceable to lack of, or poor regulations and corporate governance. He was of the opinion that this may be due to the want of directors with the will and courage to enforce regulations or due to the failure of regulatory bodies to bring violators of laid down regulations to book.

Furthermore, it needs to be reiterated that the importance of corporate governance and its application in the affairs of the aviation industry cannot be overemphasized. Some of the major challenges facing Nigeria Airlines as it concerns the issue of corporate governance include:

a. **Ownership Dilution:** Some airlines are privately owned or may be owned by the government; as such, people who may not necessarily make the best business decisions set up the operational structure. The challenge with this is numbness towards making judgment on the basis of merit. Secondly, inordinate actions like the owner of the airline initiating or cancelling scheduled flights without prior consent or decision of Flight Operations and other related operational departments in the value chain. This is indeed condemnable but regrettably do happen frequently in Nigerian aviation operations. Airline owners frequently usurp too much power and unnecessarily interfere in tasks that should be left to skilled personnel. Accountability, a key value in corporate governance, is always at variance with the tenets of corporate governance culture due to its vulnerability to abuse.

In similar development, a report by *This Day Newspaper*, observed that, some stakeholders have seen it to be out of place to accommodate an external body to serve as a moderator in their business. What is observed in most cases is that the airlines board is strictly made up of selected family members without the wealth of knowledge needed to make a success of a global and specialized industry like aviation.

This is why aviation experts strongly recommend that all business operations-related conflicts should be handled amicably while taking into consideration the capital investments of the business owners, so as to ensure its smooth running. Really, the mentality of "Me and my family Nigeria limited" as coined by Sam Adurogboye, the general manager, public relations, Nigerian Civil Aviation Authority (NCAA) which I also tagged the "I-own-it" syndrome, is seen to be a major dilemma as just a single person could take over the positions of manager, pilot, engineer and board of directors or probably a family member could be consulted for vital decisions, resulting in abrupt uninformed choices not premised on standards but on affinity. These have led to the fall of many airlines especially after fatal accidents.

b. **Political Interference:** The ICAO recommends that airlines be free from political interferences and unnecessary external pressures but Nigerian airlines have been subjected to several political interferences. For instance, there have been repeated instances of unilateral decisions to close down air spaces for the movement of Very Important Persons (VIPs) and political rallies, after bookings have been made for travels, flights have departed, and customers and / or passengers are in the air. Such flights will have to be held in the air and sometimes return back to base when permission to land is not granted. Such can result into an accident if the sector fuel gets exhausted. This is rather absurd. In other economies, separate air corridor is created for VIP movements rather than to frequently interrupt or close commercial air routes. Can you imagine the cost implications, especially fuel and numerous inconveniences to the passenger and general impact on businesses? These unnecessary interruptions of operations, will have far-reaching effects, leaving customers stranded and completely frustrated. Some even miss important business meetings leading to huge financial losses. Such disgruntled passengers can never be repeat customers if they have choices.

c.  **Training of Personnel:** When you look at the advancements in IT and the progress being made in the Artificial Intelligence field in relation to the aviation industry, you will agree with me that airlines will need to invest in regular training of their personnel so as to bring them up to speed on how to acquire the necessary skills and knowledge in technology. Along this line, training schedules and manuals as approved by NCAA, must be implemented and documented by operators in Nigeria. They are expected to receive trainings on efficiency and business process engineering, but most often than not what is obtainable is a reverse situation playing out. What I have observed is that, in most cases, firms try to cut corners by not implementing scheduled trainings due to budget in the bid to cutting costs, but in the long run this will have negative implications.

d.  I have seen this glaring corporate governance challenge play out in the Nigeria aviation space, as well as seeming indulgence and compromise by regulatory authorities. A clear example is the episode of Dana air crash. Although, the fatal accident that claimed the lives of 153 passengers changed the history of the company, the true cause of the accident was pinned down to a combination of mechanical failure of the aircraft which were due to poor maintenance culture and human error from the pilot (Premium Times, June 3, 2012). This human error, which was unintentional, arose from lack of requisite knowledge base of the personnel (pilot), and the pilot regrettably paid with his life and the life of a host of others.

In an effort to reduce the cost of operations, firms sacrifice opportunities for essential knowledge acquisition; year-on-year staff trainings take the back seat; and incompetent staff are tolerated within the system as long as flight departures and arrival (how be it very irregular schedules) are ongoing. These lead to fatal crashes, which could have been avoided by a few hours of training, retraining and refresher courses at minimal costs.

When one compares the cost of training with the cost attributable to loss of lives and properties, the difference is unimaginable. Officials who should know better unwittingly kill the airline slowly through compromises with the aim of helping management to continue posting profits at the detriment of life and investors' funds.

**Medical Fitness of Personnel:** The personnel who are expected to fly frequently just like the equipment, gadgets and machines they operate, will need to be routinely checked periodically for health stability especially because of the regular operations at high altitudes. It is recommended that cabin crew members who are trained essentially as safety assurance personnel, should undergo health checks at regular intervals for stability. All cockpit and cabin executives (pilots, co-pilots, engineers, mechanics, etc.), ought to have their health-check as priority. Their medical records must be current. When this is NOT done, there is inadvertent plan for incidences, which may eventually turn into accidents if not addressed. Such negligence will also be a perfect demonstration of "cutting corners "by management of the airlines which is tantamount to a breach of corporate governance expectations, i.e. cutting corners through avoidance of medical expenses. Nigerian Civil Aviation Authority (NCAA) has oversight responsibility over this while execution is the sole responsibility of the airline management to ensure compliance through implementation.

Failure to do this is nothing short of poor corporate governance and amounts to CUTTING CORNERS.

e. **Flight Cancellation:** Ordinarily, according to the regulations governing the aviation sector, there is a penalty for incessant flight cancellations. Nigerian airlines are well known for frequent disregard for the time and plans of their customers. Sometimes they cancel flights without prior notification. I have seen instances of people getting to know of such cancellations just minutes before the scheduled departure time when they would have arrived at the departing airport and nothing was done to compensate the customers. Operators in Nigeria lack schedule integrity.

If the airlines are subjected to schedule integrity tests and such airlines periodically perform below the minimum expectation and consequently, future schedules are not approved and or AOC is made subject to review, this will force airlines to sit up.

If the principle of responsibility and accountability are prioritized at high premiums, airline flights will not be cancelled incessantly and arbitrarily. I have seen cases of airlines cancelling a scheduled flight because it is not fully booked, and asking the passengers of the cancelled flight to join another flight. The exact reason/s for the cancellation is covered up and you will hear announcements like:
"…due to operational reasons." Even if such cost is saved in the short-run, the long-run effect of cutting such corners is detrimental to the image and schedule integrity of the airline as a whole.

f.  **Quality Assurance and Control:** Quality control, which demands for proper internal checks of every aspect of operations to ensure that all processes align with the approved authorized manual, is grossly abused in the Nigerian aviation industry. If the principles of corporate governance are rightly upheld, the person with the right competences and training is the one to handle quality control responsibilities. What I have observed over the years confirms that *"orders from above"*[11] often overturn all that the task owner has done. Business owners become dictators, disregarding the officer who should be the conscience of the airline. The officers most times feel threatened and will rather yield to the bidding of the owner in order to retain his job. This sort of behind-the-scene power play puts the life of all the passengers on board at risk. When corporate governance principles are flouted, it is an act of cutting corners which can lead to a downward slide into bankruptcy, death and destruction, and the loss of public confidence in the airline.

g.  **Hierarchy of Reporting:** In the aviation industry, we have a standard reporting procedure that promotes the principle of transparency in corporate governance. In the aircraft, the black box keeps a record of all that happens during a flight. Cockpit Voice Recorder (CVR) and Flight Data Recorder (FDR) are installed in every aircraft and are fire/explosive resistant. The pilot is expected to complete his voyage report at the completion of every successful flight in the logbook, a copy of which is sent to the airline management; another copy is sent to the CAA.

Unfortunately, this seemingly simple professional procedure is sometimes not followed especially when imagining the cost relating to the repair of the snags. Such snags are not logged or reported in the bid of cutting costs. Experience has shown however, that the only profitable way to cut costs is to ensure proper documentation and reporting to the management and appropriate authorities of a voyage experience for necessary preventive actions which is much cheaper than the massive costs of handling an accident.

# CHAPTER FIVE

# REGULATION AND POLICY IMPLEMENTATION:
## The Role of Government and Policy Effectiveness

*An unguided masquerade, no matter how strong, will surely miss its steps*

I will like you to see the aviation industry as a giant basket of eggs. You could handle the basket well, get some eggs in the incubator and get some chicken. You could sell some eggs and make money. When you think about this picture, profit and sustenance will depend on the way you handle your giant basket and the contents. If you are careless and the basket falls, the eggs will all break.

From this analogy, you can see the necessity of the appropriate guides in order to have and keep a lucrative business running. Quite a number of corporations have opened for business within the aviation industry; but as at today, most of them are either dead, or lying-in state. If you see any successful business in the aviation industry, either here or beyond our shores, that success cannot be dissociated from the effective enforcement of compliance with robust regulations and policies established to guide operations and activities within the sector. Serious operators even strive to operate above recommended minimum standards.

In the same way, we can trace failures to critical loopholes in regulatory and policy frameworks which may be insufficient, not properly implemented, and/or effectively enforced. Seemingly little festering acts of corruption, compromise, and negligence on the path of any of the key aviation stakeholders are able to wreak much havoc, which ripple effects could impact negatively on the entire aviation industry. Think about a ship and how a tiny crack could sink it.

Again, let me repeat the question we have considered before now in this discourse. We have no doubt that it is dangerous to cut corners as far as aviation regulations and policy implementations are concerned, but are there still ways of optimizing costs and increasing returns on investment without cutting corners? Ethically, whenever you stop someone from doing something you consider to be evil, you must replace it with what you consider as good. Based on this assumption, I will use this chapter to emphasize the crucial role of effectively enforced government policies and regulations to the success of a thriving aviation industry, having Nigeria in perspective. I will also give suggestions on possible ways of optimizing costs and returns on investments for the aviation industry in Nigeria, based on my experience in the field.

## ARRAY OF THE COMPLIANCE LOOPHOLES

Following the air mishap that occurred on October 29, 2018, involving the ill-fated flight JT610 – a Boeing 737 Max 8 Jet operated by Lion Air, an Indonesian Airlines Company – an incident that claimed 189 lives, preliminary findings of the National Transportation Safety Bureau (NTSB) of Indonesia, revealed that the aircraft was not airworthy following recurrent technical issues identified on the flight that the aircraft operated the previous day to the crash. In the previous day's flight, the pilot had to shut down the plane's anti-stall system to be able to make it safely to Jakarta. I have written about the compliance shortcomings that resulted in the Indonesian plane crash in the second chapter of this book, so I will like to talk about an incident involving another one of the latest Boeing passenger jets. Exactly 132 days after the JT610 crash, on

March 10, 2019, another air disaster occurred in the town of Bishoftu in Oromia region of Ethiopia. The Boeing 737 Max 8 Jet operated by the Ethiopian Airlines crashed six minutes after take-off on the flight ET302, which was enroute the Jomo Kenyatta International Airport in Nairobi, Kenya from the Bole International Airport in Addis Ababa, Ethiopia. All the 157 passengers and crew members on board died in the accident which many international sources (including reports by the BBC and CNN) have confirmed showed clear similarities with the earlier mishap involving the Lion Air flight. Data retrieved from both Cockpit Voice Recorder (CVR) and light data recorder (FDR) boxes validate this.

The aircraft was said to have been delivered to Ethiopian Airlines in November 2018, a few days after the air disaster of the Lion Air flight occurred. The same automated flight software, MCAS, is suspected to have responded to an angle of attack sensor on the outside of the plane that transmitted incorrect data, which sent the aircraft cruising into the ground.

"Hey guys, turn me around. There's something wrong with this plane", said[12] the 29-year-old Captain Yared Getachew who had logged 8000 hours of flight experience.[13]

"...flight control problems" his copilot said to the control tower. He had just received clearance to return back to the airport when the plane plummeted into the ground, killing all on board.

While it was easy for preliminary reports to blame the crash of the JT610 flight on the poor safety records of Lion Air Company, it was not easy to do that with the crash of the ET302 as many sources describe the safety standards of Ethiopian Airlines as "good," "impeccable" and "outstanding."

The B737-Max Jets have been described as the "fastest selling [planes] in history." Costing about $121 million, 5000 orders had been placed for the range of jets, and over 350 were reported to be in service globally. This sparked estimations of Boeing raking in up to $600 billion from the 737 Max range of jets alone.[14]

However, the aftermath of the incident saw the shares of the aircraft manufacturer drop speedily within 24 hours, reducing Boeing's aviation market share value by over $20 billion according to multiple sources. Within days of the crash, more than 30 countries took decisions to keep Boeing 737 Max jets out of their skies; with the U.S. Federal Aviation Administration (FAA) acting administrator, Daniel Elwell, stating that "new satellite-data and physical evidence more closely linked both crashes". The U.S. President, Donald Trump, announced the decision of the FAA to ground further operations of the aircraft type until further notice.[15]

Although, confirmed reports have it that many U.S. pilots had complained about the performance of the Boeing 737 Max Jet during flights in a federal data base. One pilot reporting, said, "…an autopilot anomaly which led to a brief nose-down situation – where the front of the aircraft [suddenly] pointed down". Another pilot, complaining about the flight manual, said, "…inadequate and almost criminally insufficient."[16]

Additionally, the New York Times also reported that, "there is no evidence that Boeing did flight-testing of [the] MCAS with erroneous sensor data, and it is not clear whether the FAA did so [either]."[17]

The unfortunate incident involving the ET302 flight, has raised a lot of questions from friends and families of the victims and from industry insiders. Questions about the regulations on the designing and testing of new aircrafts, questions about the handling of post-flight complaints by pilots about aircraft; and questions about the accident investigation processes. One uncomfortable question is whether a second air disaster (with global public outcry) was necessary to expose and draw attention to a "critical flaw" in the MCAS on Boeing's 737 Max 8 Jets. The crash eventually forced the aircraft manufacturer to review the fatal design issue which had already been repeatedly reported by pilots over the course of the preceding months.

Indeed, could robust and effective international and government regulatory policies not have helped to forestall the fate of the ET302 flight?

# CHAPTER SIX

# HISTORY AND DEVELOPMENT OF CIVIL AVIATION REGULATIONS: THE NIGERIAN EXPERIENCE

In post-colonial Nigeria, the regulation of civil aviation became the responsibility of the National (Federal) Government. As aviation in Nigeria began to thrive, forming a viable medium for boosting tourism, commerce, industry and government became the country's responsibility. There arose the need to coordinate and regulate the activities and operations of the aviation sector to meet the demands of a growing international network. This led the Federal Government of Nigeria to establish the Civil Aviation Department (CAD) in 1965, a department that was domiciled in the Federal Ministry of Transport. Following a seminar in 1988 which recommended the need to develop policies for regulating aviation operations in Nigeria. This regulatory agency created around 1989/90 became the Federal Ministry of Aviation.

According to its mission statement, it is an agency "which will be charged with safety and economic regulation of the aviation sector as well as partly handle the provision of Air Traffic Services"[18] in line with the global accepted Standards & Recommended Practices (SARPs) that had been established by the International Civil Aviation Organization (ICAO) and other international aviation bodies.

Thus, the Federal Civil Aviation Authority (FCAA) was established and tasked with the responsibility of formulating regulations and policies to guide aviation operations in the country, as well as providing air traffic control and a wide range of aeronautical services to airlines operating within and into the country.

Unfortunately, for a larger part of its existence, from inception until the early years of the new millennium, the FCAA did not enjoy the degree of operational autonomy that was needed to fulfil the official responsibilities, as the "ideal of regulatory independence was an anathema to the government." *Ibid*

The supervising ministry (the ministry of transport in the beginning, and later the ministry of aviation) and the ministers typically exert tight and rather overbearing control over the duties of the Aviation Authority; even in matters of safety and airworthiness where decisions and approvals require the inspection and recommendations of core aviation professionals. Some vital decisions are often taken unilaterally by the supervising ministry regardless of strong negative positions of responsible and skilled task-owners.

I read the accounts of some aviation historians who described this period as the blue (gloomy and uncertain) days of aviation in Nigeria. During this period, the Aviation Reforms of 1995 were proposed, which resulted in sun-setting of the Federal Civil Aviation Authority (FCAA). Thus, from 1995-1999, the functions and mandates of the defunct FCAA were split amongst two internal directorates of the Federal Ministry of Aviation – the Directorate of Safety Regulation and Monitoring (DSRAM), and the Directorate of Economic Regulation and Monitoring (DERAM).

Later, both directorates were collapsed to form the Nigerian Civil Aviation Authority (NCAA), an agency whose framework and mandates at the time was weak, incomprehensive and limited. Usually, one would expect these frantic measures of organizing and reorganizing these institutions to bring out something near perfect but the situation was not very different at any point throughout these transformations, as there were several documented instances of ministerial interferences on aviation safety and security issues. For instance, there were documented instances of already overdue aircraft maintenance schedules being further extended, and instances of aircrafts grounded due to safety concerns, which were politically cleared to fly.

One example that easily comes to mind is when an Accident Investigation Bureau (AIB) connected the July 1991 air disaster involving a Canadian registered DC8 aircraft operated by Hold- Trade Airline, one of the Hajj Operators for Nigeria Airways, while on its way to Sokoto in Nigeria from Jeddah, Saudi Arabia to one of such infringements. The aircraft, which was discovered not to have been airworthy, was signed-off as fit to fly by an operating flight engineer who had no business whatsoever in the aircraft's maintenance and repairs process. It was observed that, the FCAA's director of Airworthiness and Safety, had raised concerns about the airworthiness of the aircraft and the fact that he had not certified it as fit to fly. However, his professional view was said to have been queried and discarded by the aviation minister, who was quoted as saying, "What other certification do you require?" *Ibid* Eventually, the aircraft was cleared for operations amidst much apprehension. Everyone on board the aircraft perished in that disaster, which has been described as "the worst accident in the history of commercial aviation in Nigeria".[19]

It was also during the period of these transformations that civil aviation policy and regulation suffered its worst decline. In 1995, the sitting minister of aviation, Air Commodore Nsikak Eduok, instituted a reform that set the industry "...ten years back to the dying days of the post-colonial regulatory period in Nigeria's aviation industry."

The ministry, under the leadership of Eduok, came up with an ambiguous proposition for an "Autonomous Airport System."

I saw the handwriting on the wall like many other insightful industry players, but it is always hard to work with unwise dictators who think they are too wise. In fact, the aviation industry is not a place for dictators. Dictators, while ignorantly using their powers as they please, will turn airplanes to flying coffins.

The so-called Aviation Reforms of 1995 only succeeded in creating structures and frameworks that were not particularly compliant with globally accepted international SARPs. The airspace management schedule of the nascent FCAA was transferred to a new agency known as the Federal Airports Authority of Nigeria (FAAN). The minister also created the two directorates of the FCAA – DSRAM and DERAM – to replace the two regulatory arms of the FCAA. To make matters worse, he fired seasoned regulators and replaced them with individuals who had no experience in aviation regulation. This regressive period of steep decline has been code-named in the annals of civil aviation development in Nigeria as the "Eduokian Legacy." The immediate effect was that many international operations of the defunct Nigeria Airways were banned, and the Nigeria airspace was declared unsafe by the International Federation of Airline Pilots Association (IFALPA) in many forums. Fortunately, Capt. (Pilot) Benoni Briggs soon took over as minister and in 1999 created the Nigerian Civil Aviation Authority (NCAA) and Nigerian Airspace Management Agency (NAMA) in line with new reforms. They were to form the nucleus of a new regulatory and a principal service provider regime for civil aviation in Nigeria respectively. Change for the better was not immediate. The rot caused by the "Eduokian Legacy" had festered so deeply that it was attributed by several industry analysts to be "the remote cause that culminated in the devastating air crashes of 2005/2006 of ADC, Bellview and Sosoliso airlines".

The journey to redeeming civil aviation regulation and development in Nigeria was going to be a very difficult one, because the new regulatory regime still suffered from management stability issues, as well as the good old ministerial interferences that crippled its autonomy. In the aftermath of the 2005/2006 air disasters in Nigeria, Dr. Harold Olusegun Demuren took over as director general of the NCAA. Demuren's appointment proved to be timely as he was a seasoned aviation regulator, armed with robust knowledge of the industry, its workings and its challenges. He punctured and upturned the weak regulatory framework embodied by the NCAA Act of 1999 which had loopholes that exposed it to various degrees of external interferences even on critical issues of aviation safety and security.

In 2006, the "Civil Aviation Act" was passed into law, a victory for due process because it finally gave the NCAA the full measure of autonomy it needed to fulfill its mandates and responsibilities. The law also became the tool with which Demuren set out to enlist Nigerian civil aviation among global players. While he was director general of the NCAA from 2006-2013, Nigeria attained Federal Aviation Authority (FAA) Category 1 and passed ICAO Safety Audit. Nigeria was also invited to help some African states develop regulatory systems that are as strong as the NCAA's.

When I reflect on how things had been at my entry into the industry, and through my years of work, I have seen the civil aviation regulatory landscape survive many challenges and stages of transformation, yet it continues to emerge better than it was in the past even though it may be impossible or hard to completely eliminate the challenges of attempted political infringements, nepotism, and selfish interests propagating across some frontiers. Though far from perfect, civil aviation regulatory framework in Nigeria remains outstanding within global context. This is evident in the successes of ICAO and FAA audits since 2015.

## 1. NCAA AND NAMA: FUNCTIONS AND MANDATES CUM RESPONSIBILITIES

Earlier on, I mentioned that the aviation industry started as a baby of the British colonial government. From that time till now, there has been steady, even though troubled progress, up to a point where this child of the beginning is old enough to be trusted with responsibilities. The task of regulating civil aviation in Nigeria is principally shouldered by the Nigerian Civil Aviation Authority (NCAA) together with the Nigerian Airspace Management Agency (NAMA).

NAMA is the major aeronautical service provider. The agency is generally responsible for the provision of air navigation services throughout the Nigeria Flight Information Region. It also provides air traffic control, air navigation, charting, and consulting services across the country's 25 towered airports and two air traffic control centers.
NCAA on the other hand, has the mandate to carry out oversight functions on airports, airspaces, meteorological services, etc., as well as economic regulations of the industry. Currently, there are more than 25 airports, 30 airlines, 590 pilots, 19 flight engineers, 258 air traffic controllers (ATC), 677 aircraft maintenance engineers, 1,103 cabin crew staff and four aircraft dispatchers in Nigeria.

The Nigeria Civil Aviation Authority (NCAA) as earlier mentioned, was established with the passing into law of the Civil Aviation Act 2006 by the National Assembly of the Federal Republic of Nigeria. The functions and responsibilities of NCAA are to:

- Regulate the safety of aircraft operations, air navigation and aerodrome operations.

- Monitor the aircraft-operating environment for safety and security.

- Regulate methods of entry and the conduct of air transport businesses.

- Advice the Ministry of Aviation on policy formulation on aviation related matters.

- Balance the economic interest of operators, users of aviation services as well as the general public and the nation as a whole.

- Set aviation training standards, and approve training institutions.

- Facilitate the introduction of IATA E-Ticketing and Billing Settlement Plan (BSP).[20]

In the same vein, Act 48 of the Federal Republic of Nigeria created the Nigerian Airspace Management Agency (NAMA) in 1999. The functions of the agency upon creation are to: provide air traffic services like air traffic control; visual and non-visual aids; aeronautical telecommunication services; and related electricity supplies so as to enable public, private, business and military aircrafts fly as far as practicable and as safely as possible. The agency is also mandated to provide its services to aerodromes at major Nigerian airports, as well as the navigation services necessary for aircrafts to take-off and land, while integrating these into general air traffic within the Nigerian airspace. The agency is to control and minimize or prevent interferences with the application of appropriate apparatus used for connection with air navigation. It is their responsibility to prohibit or regulate the use of all such apparatus and display of signs and lights that could endanger aircraft and endanger other authorized users of the Nigerian airspace.

In its bid to ensure safety and efficiency, NAMA is expected to engage qualified persons in connection with air navigation, to supply meteorological information for the purpose of air navigation as may be deemed appropriate from time to time; and to provide adequate facilities and personnel for effective security of navigational aids outside the airport perimeters. NAMA would also create conditions for the development, in the most efficient and economic manner, of air transport services; and procure, install and maintain adequate communication, navigation, surveillance and air traffic management facilities at all airports in Nigeria.

Additionally, NAMA is empowered to: "ensure an effective co-ordination in the use of Nigeria's airspace in line with established standards and procedures," "ensure the co-ordination at all levels of decisions relating to airspace management and air traffic control in Nigeria," "hold meetings with the armed forces on Nigeria's international obligations as they relate to civil and military co-ordination;" "promote familiarization visits by civil and military personnel to air traffic service units;" "maintain permanent liaison with the civil air traffic services units and all relevant air defense units, in order to ensure the daily integration or segregation of civil and military air traffic operating within the same or immediately adjacent portions of the Nigerian airspace. Other duties include employing civil or military radars as necessary;" "…obviate the need for civil aircraft to obtain special air defense clearance;" "…take necessary steps to prevent, as far as possible, penetration of control airspace by any aircraft, civil or military without coordination with the air traffic control unit concerned;" "…encourage research and development relating to all aspects of the Nigerian airspace designed to improve air safety;" "…undertake systems engineering development and implementation for communications, navigation and surveillance and air traffic

Management;" "…charge for services provided by the Agency;" "…co- ordinate the implementation of search and rescue services;" and "…discharge the operational, technical and financial air traffic service commitments arising from Nigeria's membership of international organizations and other air navigation agencies."

## 2. REGULATORY SHORTCOMINGS AND LIMITATIONS

Despite the numerous reforms that have helped to foster aviation development in Nigeria to its current enviable international status, I can still list, without stopping to pause, some of the shortcomings, challenges and limitations that yet hinder the aviation agencies of government in gearing towards their full potentials and many who are vast in the knowledge of the field will agree with me. One of the numerous shortcomings I have voiced out any time the opportunity presents itself is the act of not sufficiently enforcing compliance to aviation programmes by the regulatory agencies of government. Another is outdated policies and porous bilateral agreements. It is important to always remember that economic regulations need to be revamped to meet up with the dynamic transformations and realities of the modern age.

I have also noticed the seeming negligence of the government regulatory authority in the areas of thorough regular safety and financial auditing. It would be great if the process of paying the insurance compensation benefits of victims of aviation accidents to their legal next-of-kin is without hiccups and road blocks. I also noticed poor engagement among aviation stakeholders across all levels. Imagine a football team where some players would rather do what they like because of their perceived power and influence, instead of working as a team to win together. Many of these issues have been discussed repeatedly and extensively at the Aviation Roundtable (ART), the foremost association of aviation stakeholders in Nigeria.

The Aviation Roundtable brings together regulators, airline operators, travel management companies, consultants, pilots, safety engineers, travellers, etc., and its recommendations are widely published and passed on to the seat of government and agencies of civil aviation in Nigeria. Most of the issues raised, the ideas explored and the insights provided, sometimes seem to be of little or no value, of no consequence and sparingly heeded. They are generally perceived as criticism of government but of course, they are usually genuine concerns devoid of prejudice.

## ADDRESSING THE CRITICAL ISSUES IN AVIATION REGULATIONS

History has continued to suggest that civil aviation cannot be successful by accident.

We have to be deliberate, work on effective policy and regulatory measures, start by *'talking the right talk'*, and then progress to *'walking the right talk.'* I'm talking about policy development and policy implementation beyond mere paperwork and nice speeches. Looking beyond our shores, I have noticed that civil aviation regulation / policy development remains the frontline agenda of a progressive global aviation industry.

Despite the challenges, I want us to remember the popular saying, "Rome was not built in a day;" and another one, "The journey of a thousand miles begins with a step." So, for our industry, I am confident that there are better days ahead because by continuing to identify and objectively analyze these emerging challenges within a progressively inclusive stakeholders framework, and then evaluating recommendations without biases, prejudice and sentiments, Nigeria's civil aviation industry will rise to a position of global reckoning in the not too distant future.

# CHAPTER SEVEN

## LOGISTICS: Hippos and Gazelles

W hen I was a child, I would look at the sky and admire birds and their freedom to fly. The sky, without obstacles, above mountains, valleys and hills and seas and other limitations, gives the aviation industry an enormous growth potential that no other transport system can boast of.

The growing demand for air travel has resulted in astronomical rise in the need for more efficient aircrafts. Companies like, Boeing, Airbus, Embraer, Bombardier, Comac and other major commercial aircraft manufacturers are finding it difficult to meet the everincreasing demands from airline companies.

The rush for customers and profit has changed the dynamics to the point that the gazelles are dancing with the hippos in a marshland. The plain land of Ogbona in Edo State overlooks the marshland where hippos in years past used to play, fight and mate. The gazelles watch as these animals wage war of life and death. One day, the hippos were so carried away that one of the gazelles joined them in the game. What happened? The gazelle discovered that the difference between him and the hippos was how the hippos were built and not the environment. The hippos were built to last. They were built with internal strength and strategic capabilities. While the gazelle admired the joy of the hippos, it was important not to forget that the hippos were different. In this game of the hippos, there is no room to cut-corners.

There are three factors that underpin this experience.

The first is that the animals are not identical, but possess different capabilities. The gazelle cannot obtain or copy the capabilities of a hippo. The second arises from the aforementioned. If an animal is to achieve competitive advantage, it will do so on the basis of capabilities that its rivals do not have or have difficulties in obtaining.

The foundation of this analogy is not solely about competences and strategic capabilities but how these are used to produce at lower cost or generate superior performance. Airlines are cutting corners due to inability to continually improve cost efficiency and poor understanding of their value chain, value network, activity mapping, and benchmarking.

Different writers, managers and consultants have used various terminologies to explain the pitfall in jumping into business or a business route without full understanding of the cost implications and sustainability road map. Just like the gazelles, some airlines have threshold capabilities but not core competences. This lack of combination of dedication to cost efficiency, tenacity, time to train, demanding levels of competition and a will to win is the breeding ground for cutting corners.

Cutting corners exist when executing a strategy that requires toolkit of competencies built around a knowledge workforce is carried out, accepted and approved by quacks. The knowledge of customers, coupled with innovative customers' solutions, is behind the attractiveness and survival of major international airlines. In addition, it is the airline's innovative capability that produces a robust pipeline of products, customers and value superiority. This has justified the claims of one of the major aircraft manufacturers, Airbus, in its latest Global Market Forecast which estimates that the world's overall passenger aircraft inventory will double from 17,739 in 2013 to more than 36,500 by 2032. Though other major players in the aircraft manufacturing industry have not said anything, recent activities from some aircraft buyers have corroborated this projection.

Will innovation and quick fix lead to cutting corners?

To emerge world-class is not a product of cutting corners. It is not an idle or boastful claim, rather the output of commitment to work and cost differential.

Hippos and gazelles are about management cost (risk) as a strategic capability. It is not all that looks great that is great. Understanding risk and cost efficiency based on an airline's inherent power is also the basis for achieving competitive advantage. Industry watchers have observed that there has been a heightened pressure on manufacturers to produce planes more quickly, efficiently, and profitably. There has equally been an end user input in the design and manufacturing of aircrafts as buyers not only buy just what is available.

Aircraft manufacturers now face challenges bothering on manufacturing of lighter aircraft with lower fuel consumption using materials sourced from a geographically diverse supplier base. The thrust of this perspective is to manage cost at customer levels but forgetting that customers do not value product features at any price. The behaviour of customers is sometime erratic. If the price rises too high, they sacrifice value and opt for lower price. So, the challenge is to ensure that an appropriate level of value is offered at an acceptable price. This means that everyone is technically forced to keep costs as low as possible, consistent with the value to be provided. The gazelles who lack the power of keeping the cost lower, watch as customers switch products or invite hippos to feast.

Competing airlines will continually require the driving down of costs because competitors will be trying to reduce their costs so as to over-price their rivals while offering similar value. In this situation, if cost is to be managed effectively, attention has to be paid to key cost drivers.

Cutting cost is achieved through economies of scale especially when the high cost of operation needs to be recovered over a high volume of flight and full capacity. In addition, cutting cost is obtainable in distribution or marketing of which location and economic viability is a factor. Operations design also influences cost rather than corner. Efficiency gained in operations design enables labour productivity yield and working capital utilization. Experience is key to cost efficiency and there is evidence that cumulative experience gained by an organization and its unit costs shape the experience curve.

With airport logistics, corner cutting is not cost cutting.

The planning and control of all resources and information that create value for customer utilization at the airport is inevitable. When you think about this very well, you will realize that the concept of airport logistics is very broad. Logistics and transportation methods mainly include water, land, and air transportation. Thus, air transportation is an important part of the aviation logistics process because of its safety, reliability, wide range of spatial radiation, and long-range transportation effectiveness. Therefore, the logistics industry is an important part of a country's economy because freight volume can effectively reflect the level of business activities in that country or region. Aviation logistics relies on air transportation combined with other modes of transport, primarily road transportation, rail and sea through intermodal connections to provide consumers with a series of door-to-door services. Modern logistics deploy information technology techniques to connect the sender (shipper) to the recipient of the goods (the consignee). Aviation logistics is an uninterrupted process and the personnel of this network are connected by real time information systems that enable all parties to share information and be able to monitor goods from one point to another. Through this service, the supply chain, the flow of goods and the exchange of information are monitored. At the risk of overgeneralization, the elements are relatively missing in the Nigerian context. This explains why the domestic flights are nightmares and unprepared for the market. Taking a leap from international cargo (which constitutes 75% of total), Europe-Middle East-Africa-Asia axis, Turkey being geographically located in the centre of this axis, is placed at a very favorable position for passenger transfers and cargo trans-shipment. Considering Cost, Insurance and Freight (CIF) costs, speed, and security benefits of air logistics, 40% of the total world cargo is transported by air. Therefore, aviation logistics (which is one of the top three emerging sectors in the 21st century economy) is gaining more importance, recognition and attention globally. With the concept of "Just-In-Time" (JIT) logistics, "time" has become an important factor. According to IATA, "goods that, due to their nature, weight, dimensions and/or value, may have specific requirements on packaging, labelling, documentation and handling through the transport chain...

Transportation of these goods are addressed through specific regulations that must be followed when preparing, offering, accepting and handling the cargo."

The urgency of some materials such as radiopharmaceuticals for medical diagnosis and handling of high-value goods such as technological products and valuable commodities such as money and jewelry, make air transport the best mode. Some of these **items include dangerous goods, live animals,** perishable cargo, wet cargo, time and temperature sensitive products. Most of these survive only when logistics is handled perfectly and efficiently. Other items under this category are perishables like cut flowers, vegetables, Aircraft On Ground (AOG) spares, currencies, precious goods like gold and diamond and ammunitions among others. These goods, because of how special their nature is, require short delivery time and aviation logistics facilitates the seamless process. Aviation logistics has rapidly developed in recent time, thus, air transportation is being preferred and used more than other transportation modes. Aviation logistics is at the hub of all airline multi-sector activities.

However, given the increasingly high demand for air logistics and the poor experience on past services, this sector must strengthen its service supply chain to expand its market and revenue base. The increasing demand for people to travel for business, meetings, vacations, visits to family and friends together with lots of goods, has resulted in a steady increase in air cargo transportation over the past decades. Trans-shipment airports do cause delays, damage/loss of goods and create unnecessary bottlenecks in the process.

The airport runs a complicated system with many time-critical-processes as well as different actors with diverse and contradicting objectives. To increase predictability and punctuality at the airport, "Collaborative Decision Making" (CDM) process was introduced. CDM, initiated by Euro-Control has been implemented to different levels at several airports of the world. But access to all the information alone will not make the planning more efficient. It is also important to know how to handle every new information and the growing amount of information makes planning and decision making more complex.

The increased information gathering from CDM is one of the reasons why Airport Logistics (AL) project started in the spring of 2006. The project is the collaboration between the LFV Group (the Swedish civil aviation administration) and Linköping University. The Air Navigation Services division (ANS) at LFV had identified some bottlenecks in the system, especially at airports, but they were not able to deduce the precise causes. The quest to unravel this unknown, led to the idea of a research project at the university in 2006.

## CHARACTERISTICS OF AVIATION LOGISTICS SERVICE SUPPLY CHAIN

The three known characteristics of the aviation logistics service supply chain are:

a.  **Customer Involvement:** A high degree of customer involvement is the first characteristic of this supply chain because unlike ordinary supply chains, the starting and finishing points of the aviation logistics service supply chain involve customers. Whereas in ordinary production logistics supply chains, customers only play a role at the end of the supply chain.

In aviation, logistics service supply chain begins with one customer and ends with another customer. Therefore, the information systems established in aviation logistics are required to connect with customers at the starting and finishing points to complete simultaneous information exchange on two-way basis. The response of customers should be received immediately in real time. Thus, customers' participation plays a decisive role in completing the logistics process of the aviation logistics service supply chain.

b. **Customer-Driven Demands:** The aviation logistics service supply chain is driven by the needs of customers. If the needs of upstream customers and supply sources are lacking in aviation logistics, then all aspects of its supply chain will be missing their service targets. Therefore, this supply chain is established in line with customer demands, and its operations must be implemented based on these needs.

c. **Rapid Response:** The characteristics of the aviation logistics service supply chain are similar to those of a responsive supply chain. The most evident characteristic is the uncertainty of market demand, and thus rapid response is essential. Two factors are considered with regards to market demands in Aviation Logistics. The first is diverse customer base and the second is high transportation costs. Ordinarily, production logistics can be prioritized to implement inventory management with a high degree of control for demands. In contrast to aviation logistics service supply chain, quick response may become unnecessary.

Basically, the objectives of the airport logistics project are to develop a complete picture of all the processes and activities at and around the airport as well as analyze the usage of all these resources, to find optimal solution for the entire airport, rather than solutions optimized for an individual player.

If you really look at the operations in an airport, you will find out that a large number of players are involved on every flight. A lot goes on to get the airplane airborne, a lot goes on to keep the plane safe and passengers comfortable in the air, and a lot goes on to ensure safe landing, passage of passengers and their luggage, and readiness for the next flight. The aviation industry's processes are time critical. These are the main reasons for the complexity of airport logistics where most of the players are involved in the turnaround process. It starts when an aircraft touches down and goes on until it takes off again. This process also connects to other processes on airside, at air traffic control (ATC) and inside the terminal and this makes it one of the main processes that influence the smooth running of airport logistics. Any compromise at any level of these processes will be cutting corners.

Furthermore, the airlines' primary planning goal or focus is to achieve the most efficient transportation of passengers and cargoes between various airports. For this to be possible, airlines will need to offer their services at airports where these services are requested. They also need to have an appropriate fleet of aircrafts as well as an effective schedule in order to meet these needs while flying the routes that are most profitable.

It is hard to define an ideal solution for airport operations because this would depend on what is adjudged as "ideal". If the mission is to have an airport that is efficient, available, robust, safe, secure, profitable and environmentally friendly, then some of these parameters could be contradictory. Nevertheless, an airport usually aims to fulfill all these parameters.

Some special indicators known as *Airport Performance Indicators (API)* are used to measure whether a criterion is fulfilled or not. In order to create an effective flow of passengers, cargo and airplanes to meet and function in the airport, a well-developed infrastructure and support organization is necessary. The air traffic control authorities have the main objective of guaranteeing safe air traffic, but they are also responsible for managing the total flow of aircraft to reduce congestion and delays. This is called Air Traffic Management (ATM). Schedule design is a strategic planning process in which schedules of flights for serving potential markets are determined. Assigning an aircraft to various sectors/ legs of a flight is described as aircraft routing. Since an aircraft must carry out routine maintenance at periodic intervals, aircraft routing also involves planning of time and place for such maintenance.

In addition to managing the aircraft fleet, an airline operator must plan the aircraft crew rotation, training, and welfare. The most extensively studied topic in this area is crew scheduling, which consists of creating minimum-cost crew schedules (called Crew Pairings) and the assignment of the schedules to individual crew members (called Crew Assignment). Clearly, the capacities of the logistics processes (in addition to the capacity of an infrastructure, such as runways) at the airport will highly influence the operational plans of airline operators. In the context of airport logistics, the most relevant operation of Air Traffic Management (ATM) is Air Traffic Flow Management (ATFM) which deals with coordinating traffic flows at national, regional and international levels. The decisions made in ATFM, is deployed in regulating air traffic globally. Some measures in ATFM include re-routing (i.e. choosing alternative routes for aircrafts), metering (i.e. controlling the aircraft's arrival time), and ground holding (i.e. delaying the departure of flights in order to avoid overload).

## PERSONNEL INVOLVED IN AIRPORT LOGISTICS

The personnel or units involved in turn-around processes include:

a.  Air Traffic Control (ATC): separates the aircrafts to prevent air collisions and manage an efficient traffic flow.

b.  Airport Companies: responsible for providing safe, secure and environmentally friendly atmosphere at the airport and for providing all that is needed for airport departures and arrivals.

c. Aviation Handling Companies: handle all travel formalities at the airport especially where the airline does not have physical presence like check-in points, catering services, etc based on agreed contract with the principal airline.

d. Airlines: operate aircrafts for commercial purposes, earn commercial payloads in line with travel needs and deliver customer satisfaction.

e. Aviation Authorities: supervise and see to it that all the rules are obeyed by personnel, passengers and cargo owners. Their role is to promote safe, cost effective and environment friendly civil aviation.

f. Airport Security: ensure safe and secure environment for lives and properties of travelers within and immediate airport environment.

During turn-around, activities carried out by the handling companies include, loading and offloading of baggage, catering, cleaning, fueling and de-icing processes.

It is instructive to view the Airport Transportation System (ATS) as a network having value linkage flows. The commercial payload (passenger, cargo, mail, etc) moving from point to point form the value in ATS.

The overall efficiency of the complex system is a function of every single participant in the network. To maximize the overall efficiency, the operations performed by one actor should be made available to all other actors. This is the core concept of Collaborative Decision Making (CDM).

I'm sure you still remember my analogy of the aviation industry as a chain that needs to avoid weak links or broken links as much as possible. In collaborative decision-making (CDM), airlines, airports, handling companies and ATC should all have access to the same information within the system. An operator should be able to influence decisions, including decisions made by another operator, which will affect its operations in the system.

Furthermore, Collaborative Decision Making (CDM) will provide solutions for navigation, surveillance and control of aircraft, which is superior to the radar-based systems in use today. These technical advances result in an increased amount of information availed to each actor in the ATS, which if correctly applied, should lead to improved use of resources, as well as reduced delays and waiting times.

One thing to note is that the growing amount of information would lead to a mounting complexity in the decision making process as the number of options available for the decision makers grow. Thus, improvement in efficiency requires that each operator has the ability to handle and utilize the new information. The goal of airport logistics is to utilize and process the information made available through CDM to achieve efficient resource management.

Airport logistics does not only include managing the pure airport processes, but also the relevant air traffic management and airline processes as well.

Reducing the turn-around time of each aircraft has been one way of increasing the capacity in the ATS. A lot goes on during the turnaround period: passengers and baggage have to be unloaded, the aircraft has to be cleaned, sometimes fumigation is necessary, the aircraft would also need to be refueled. The toilets have to be cleaned, waste bin emptied and the food supplies re-stocked. Sometimes, snow and ice have to be removed before the aircraft can be allowed to take-off again. The efficiency of each of these processes has a direct impact on the turn-around time of the aircraft. The turn-around process is essential in the airport system, as most of the other relevant processes and activities connect to each other during the turn-around.

The critical path for an aircraft, that is, the activities that are critical for the turn-around time of that particular aircraft, can be calculated depending on the availability of all the resources needed. However, at most major airports, several turn-around processes occur simultaneously and many of these processes depend on shared resources, like fuel vehicles, cleaning staff and baggage handlers. If any of these are late to a specific aircraft, the turn- around time for that aircraft might suffer.

Some airport objectives like availability, effectiveness, profitability, robustness, safety and security or environment friendliness are used to find solutions that are propitious for the entire airport which is the aim of airport logistics. In most cases, an airport has the ambition to fulfil all these objectives, and some to a certain degree. This is often complicated as some of these objectives are contradicting. To make the situation even more complex, the goals between the different operators at the airport are sometimes also conflicting. Think about trying to make customers/passengers happy, and trying to be thorough with all the checks that are needed to ensure that both airplane and crew are fit to fly. Sometimes being thorough would take more time than usual with some degree of inconvenience (and customers might not be happy).

## PROBLEM IN AVIATION LOGISTICS

The major issues in the development of aviation logistics service supply chain are:

a.  **The improvement of control over cargo terminals:** Multiple operators/operations are involved in a single cargo terminal which culminates in complex control issues. If airlines allow air cargo terminals to operate inefficiently, then the aviation logistics service supply chain will be negatively impacted. The origin and termination points of air transportation are the cargo terminals of airports according to the composition and operation of the aviation logistics service supply chain. The two airport cargo terminals play two completely different roles in the aviation logistics chain. The first is the freight terminal for receiving goods, whereas the second is the freight terminal for delivery. Both locations are key points for connecting air and road transportation. However, airlines have low investment in airport cargo terminals at present, and their control is very weak being tenants in most cases.

b.  **Competitiveness:** Competition in the original aviation logistics market has become intense. In recent years, economic data, such as air cargo volume and postal traffic, have been recorded, thereby attracting numerous investors to join the aviation logistics industry. Enterprises are mainly interested in profits and in products with the same quality. Hence, products with low prices frequently dominate the market.

c.  **Service products and business types:** The types of services that aviation logistics enterprises can provide are relatively simple and limited. Traditional air transport only requires the completion of point-to-point operations from one airport to another. However, such air transport rarely provides customized services in response to customer demands. For that reason, high revenues cannot be produced because of a decline in the bargaining power of aviation logistics enterprises. Likewise, the short service chain and low added value result in low profits.

d. **Internal information sharing platforms:** Nearly all airlines have built their own information systems. However, communicating and sharing horizontal information among members of the aviation logistics industry is difficult due to differences in their information development systems, use of information processing technologies, and incompatibility of equipment. Thus, logistics information sharing platforms across the entire industry are lacking, and this affects the efficiency of the aviation logistics industry. These issues must be understood by aviation enterprises so as to develop favorable strategies to solve these key issues and provide services that can meet customers' needs.

## SOLUTIONS TO AVIATION LOGISTIC PROBLEMS

The solutions to the issues stated above, which have so far hindered smooth operation in aviation logistics industry include:

a. Aviation logistics enterprises should increase the types of logistics products provided. They must also offer customized solutions to key customers to increase their profits. Globally, uniform standard should be formulated by the aviation logistics industry to provide strategies for localized or customized services according to the needs of the region or specific customers.
b. It is necessary to build internal information sharing platforms in the aviation logistics industry. However, in the process of docking information systems in the aviation logistics industry, the daily operations of companies become transparent as operational data may expose company operations, and the appearance of technical problems can lead to the disclosure of corporate strategy. As a result of this, system vulnerabilities should be checked first and a professional information technology team should evaluate the risk of system information leakage before setting up information

platforms or linking information systems among aviation logistics enterprises. Moreover, aviation logistics enterprises should separate internal from external system networks to avoid divulging sensitive information to competitors and information systems must be reviewed and enhanced immediately after discovering such vulnerabilities.

c.  Since the low-quality operating status of cargo terminals seriously affects the overall operations of the aviation logistics service supply chain, airlines should increase their investment in cargo terminals to strengthen control of aviation cargo terminals in order to improve the convenience of using such terminals.

d.  Aviation logistics enterprises should exert extreme caution when constructing automation equipment to increase input in cargo terminals. For example, cargo tracking can be achieved through radio-frequency identification technology and manual information entry can be eliminated.

e.  In terms of establishing the core operating mechanism, aviation logistics enterprises can replace the original manual operation mode with automated operations (3D warehouses or automated sorting systems) that will improve the efficiency of storage and package of cargoes. And it would reduce the wrong delivery of cargoes and waste of resources. The amount of completed work per unit of time can be increased; costs can be reduced, leading to an increase in the total revenue.

f.  The aviation logistics industry must enhance its own competitiveness to withstand peer pressure and remain in the market without being eliminated. To win the market with more competitive products, enterprises must respond quickly to avoid failure to response due to constant changes in the market.

g.  Favorable prices, large aircraft fleets, and a wide route network are important components for increasing the competitiveness of aviation enterprises. If these components are completely reformed, then the investment of aviation enterprises in infrastructure and operational efficiency must be expanded to meet the customers' needs.

h. Aviation logistics enterprises can also organize strategic partnerships so as to avoid the negative impact of increasing competition amongst them.

In addition to the aforementioned, as the global and domestic air cargo markets are gradually expanding, the volume of aviation cargo traffic has increased and aviation cargo enterprises have grown. Therefore, with the increasingly intense competition among aviation cargo enterprises, traditional air transportation can no longer satisfy customers' demand for services. Aviation logistics enterprises must strengthen their service supply chain in order to expand their market. To date, the concept of aviation logistics service supply chain has been developed and many problems have arisen in the practice of aviation cargo enterprises. As a result, it was found that one of the things making logistics at an airport complex is the large number of actors involved, as well as the many activities that are sensitive to time. One of such processes is the turnaround process which is a key process for airport logistics. In addition to maintaining an active participation in the marketplace, the core operating mechanism of aviation logistics enterprises will determine the direction and speed of their development during the period of long-term strategic development. Hence, aviation logistics enterprises should continually try to understand the potential needs of customers and control and anticipate changes in market demands in order to avoid service elimination.

# CHAPTER EIGHT

# CREW MANAGEMENT IN THE NIGERIAN AVIATION INDUSTRY

If travelling as a whole were to be a kingdom, air travel would be the king among others. It is the fastest means of connecting places while utilizing a complex combination of technological, human and organisational resources. Even if a country does not have a coast or good roads, it must certainly have a sky.

Think of a palace of a prosperous kingdom. Elegant men and women are always responsible for the reception of guest(s), and also the safety, comfort, and welfare of all persons in the palace including guests. These palace men and women are trained to ensure the similitude of exquisite comfort, a kind that would remind the residents or guests that 'this is a palace, not an ordinary comfortable home'. Their majestic treatment offers such reminiscing special feelings to the receiver. To the aviation industry, the exercise is similar.

In the aviation industry, the cockpit crew and cabin crew consist of elegant men and women responsible for the reception of everyone boarding a flight and ensuring the flight arrives at its destination safely. The crew members are sometimes mistakenly classified as one and the same, but this is far from being so. Experiences have shown that a successful flight requires the perfect interplay between the cockpit and the cabin crew.

The cockpit crew consists of two pilots especially on short-haul flights: the commander of the flight and the first officer.

One pilot serves as, "Pilot flying" and the other as, "Pilot monitoring." The former flies the aircraft while the latter watches the instruments and provide all essential supports. The cabin crew is everyone that provides one service or the other on board of an aircraft outside the cockpit. Flight attendants, senior flight attendants, pursers, and onboard chefs, etc. They are all a part of the team that is responsible for the well-being of passengers on a flight. Thus, while the cockpit crew makes travel by air (among all other means of transportation) an experience not to forget very quickly, the cabin crew provide warm reception and friendly disposition on board, including serving of meals and refreshments; providing personalized entertainment equipment; and constantly being courteous, friendly and cultured. These make air travel quite pleasurable and memorable.

The responsibilities of cabin executives are highly demanding both physically and emotionally and there is a high degree of obligation and expectation required. Their activities spread up to emotion, empathy and diplomacy. Crew procedures are highly regarded in the aviation industry.

## THE CABIN CREW ORDEAL

Aviation industry across the African continent has experienced sporadic growth in recent years with older legacy operators competing fiercely with the new low-cost players. In Nigeria particularly, the good thing about this expansion is the wider choice of airlines, many of them flying with new aircrafts which have helped to improve the country's image on air safety in the wake of a spate of crashes some years back. No airline can function without its crew members.

The key role of an airline crew member is to ensure on-board safety and welfare of passengers. One of the major competitive strategies utilized by the commercial aviation industry is ensuring quality service delivery and passenger satisfaction. The crew must be thoughtful, discerning, sensitive and socially intelligent and interactive individuals at their work place. Thus, efforts should be made by the airline operator not to cut corners but to ensure quality welfare provision for its crew members, as frustrated and aggrieved crew members cannot render the world-class services required.

Rude and unfriendly attitudes of the crew executive can have adverse effect on the image and reputation of the airline and erode its brand and market value. This is understandable since the cabin crew is an important part of the human face of the airlines.

Several stakeholders have blamed most of the air crashes in Nigeria to managerial failure on the part of the aviation agencies. Sometimes when I see the level of unprofessionalism displayed by the ground crew of some airlines from check-in counters to the tarmac, I wonder if such airline representatives forget they are faces of their companies (and even if they forget that they are) they should understand the implication of customer dissatisfaction to their brand survival.

I have also observed that corruption and bureaucratic inconsistencies have adversely affected this industry when compared to other countries. Statistics have indicated that there are over 500 unemployed indigenous pilots and cabin crew personnel. It is on record that Nigerian airlines prefer to employ expatriate pilots and cabin crew personnel, pay them higher emoluments, which come along with outrageous holiday allowances and other welfare packages. The Nigerian airline operators and other aviation organisations also employ expatriate engineers, technical advisers, flight dispatchers, commercial directors and even financial managers just to mention but a few. The reasons for the reluctance of airlines to hire local personnel like pilots includes their perceived lack of experience and exposure. The expatriates are usually more perceived as possessing superior technical knowledge, better devotion and loyalty.

## COCKPIT AND CABIN CREW ILLUSION

Despite the huge potential and prospects in the aviation industry, its training institutions such as the Nigerian College of Aviation Technology (NCAT), Zaria, the International Aviation College, Ilorin and other authorized aviation training organizations in the country, are not yet top-notch platforms for advanced trainings after the initial ab initio trainings. They have not been able to measure up with their foreign counterparts and this has led to lack of requisite experience among indigenous cabin crew members.

I have seen a lot of people who had to travel out of the country to get world-class refresher/up-to-date training because they can't get it here. This, by implication, takes away significant foreign exchange from the country and has resulted in substantial capital flight from the aviation industry. The airline operators pay more than double what they would ordinarily pay a Nigerian pilot in order to engage a foreign expatriate. There are also additional disadvantages attached to the employment of a foreigner, such as a business class tickets whenever he/she travels, payment of accommodation, security and overseas vacation travels. Many Nigerian carriers have however become averse to engaging foreign expatriate pilots and other technical personnel. The indigenous pilots would continue in their disadvantaged positions except adequate measures are put in place to correct the training deficiencies and appropriate resources are channelled towards research and development in the nation's institutions. Sometimes the justification for employment of foreign experts in the aviation industry is the likelihood of Nigerian pilots gaining on the job experience and building the capacity to take over, but the big question is, are there advanced training institutions / organizations where both the foreign and the indigenous pilots can do their checks locally?

Where this is accomplished, it will bring about a sustainable way of developing human capacity. There have been advocacy efforts by various interest groups to convince the Nigerian government to give incentives such as tax exemptions or tax holidays to airline operators. I believe that if such incentives are given to airlines, they will be able to absorb on the average, ten (10) or more Nigerian pilots and train them with the requisite skills.

On the other hand, one thing that is not uncommon is that many Nigerian youths who trained as pilots as well as cabin crew members and obtained certificates in our national institutions, do not possess the necessary funding to go for type rating overseas trainings and therefore languish at home, waiting for jobs that may not come. Some even abandon their dream of becoming a pilot to do other things just to survive.

Human capital in the aviation industry remains very critical despite the advancement in technology. Irrespective of the huge investments in sophisticated technology which includes allied facilities such as the use of robots, computerized and artificial intelligence and so on, the role of human resources in terms of the cabin and cockpit crew remains pivotal or critical in the quest to ensure world class operation.

Unfortunately, majority of the cabin and cockpit crew members feel they are not really appreciated. We can then imagine what would happen if an incompetent, disgruntled or unhappy worker is to supervise or handle the sophistication in the cockpit / cabin of an airline. Disaster certainly looms, as the attitude or the mood of the worker would definitely affect the way he or she operates the device.

The simple fact we can deduce from this is that for a world-class operation to be achieved in the industry, a high premium must be placed on training and retraining, better remuneration and general welfare of workers. Incessant strikes by workers have been credited to the poor working conditions in the aviation industry and I believe that airline operators need to take proactive steps to create the right working conditions to motivate their workers. This will help to keep the Nigerian sky safer for the flying public. Reports have shown that in the last five years, the Nigerian airspace has remained relatively safe with no air accident recorded, and much of this credit goes to the service of tireless crew members.

Also worthy of commendation and appreciation are the men and women of Nigeria's aviation regulatory agencies, airport services, air traffic control, ground handlers, security, intelligence, immigration, customs, police, and airlines working assiduously to maintain a zero-accident industry. This great feat has also been applauded by the global aviation regulators organization such as the International Civil Aviation Organisation (ICAO) and the International Air Transport Association (IATA).

In the last two years, it appears to me that the plight of the Nigerian aviation employee (especially cabin crew members), rather than improving, is getting worse even though steps are being taken by the government through investments aimed at improving the state of infrastructure in Nigerian airports. But our industry thrives primarily on viable airlines and this is where the snag lies. One functional aircraft in the air can keep about 150 workers or more active. At present, Nigeria lacks strong, profitable and competitive domestic airlines. Existing carriers like Aero Contractors, Arik Air, and Medview Airline have depleting aircraft fleets and are declaring hundreds of staff redundant.

Some foreign airlines are either making Nigerian workers casual staff or laying them off in preference for their nationals owing to Nigeria's weak labour laws which fail to protect the local workforce. Thus, Nigeria's aviation sector requires a local content law that is a bit like the one operating in oil and gas industry and maritime if it hopes to cut down on most of the challenges faced by its local workforce.

At present, foreign airlines are having a field day flying into Nigeria's various airports unchallenged as Nigeria lacks capacity to reciprocate its over 88 Bilateral Air Service Agreements (BASA) signed with foreign countries. There should be a way to make it mandatory for all foreign airlines operating in Nigeria to have a certain number of Nigerian pilots and cabin crews on their fleet. This will go a long way in creating new jobs for Nigerian professionals and it will cut down on some of the capital flights linked to foreign carriers. I am not an advocate of any form of dictatorship in this industry, but there should be policies that discourage the hiring of expatriates by private airline operators to positions that can be filled by competent Nigerians.

As a nation, we have to make a conscious and deliberate decision to train and retrain the men and women that will take full advantage of growth opportunities in the global aviation and aerospace industries in the future. There must be collaboration and constant interaction between the industry and academia to better train talent and meet the skill shortage in the aviation industry. Nigerian airlines, airports management, training institutions and regulatory agencies, have to work together along the entire value chain to achieve this goal.

I strongly recommend that Nigerian Civil Aviation Authority (NCAA) should focus more on economic regulations in the entire value chain especially on general financial health of the airlines especially its workers, just as it is doing with safety regulations. Owing staff wages up to six months or more is cutting corners and encouraging accidents. The psyche of the crew is directly proportional to its diligence on board. Most local airlines do not last up to their 10th anniversary mainly due to the financial recklessness of owner managers in particular and poor treatment of workers. The latter is often grossly underestimated. Treating crew members with contempt has huge consequences ranging from security, to economics. For instance, it is suspected that until its takeover by AMCON, poorly paid cabin crew and ground handling staff of Arik Air were allegedly colluding with or facilitating the smooth operation of drug barons, human traffickers and stowaways on the airline's aircraft to overseas countries. This act of criminality is condemnable and must not be allowed to thrive in an industry such as aviation because of its multiplier effects on the entire nation at large especially at this time when security issues have become a major challenge.

I have observed over the years that the aviation industry in Nigeria lacks enough opportunities for human capacity development for young graduates. Basic training only, is tantamount to one year experience repeated many years after and there will be no improvement. Training and retraining results into gaining and regaining. Training will impact productivity of personnel that is adequately polished and project the image of the company positively. Knowledge sharing among colleagues will also be an added advantage. Hence, this is a wake-up call for every stakeholder in the aviation sector to engage in robust human capacity development. It is a necessary and sufficient condition to sustain a world class cockpit and cabin crew experience to suit the contemporary corporate world.

# CHAPTER NINE

# CUSTOMER CARE: The Challenge

I believe that any business that fails to recognize the need for deliberate, considerate and ethical treatment of customers in the provision of services is not ready to survive for a long time. This is even more important in the aviation industry because the industry clientele are majorly elites of the society.

Positive "Word of mouth" by one satisfied customer could be of far more value in recommending your brand than millions spent on adverts. Maya Angelou once said "People will forget what you said, people will forget what you did, but people will never forget how you made them feel."

The customer's experience of your service is one great platform for the growth of your business. It could take months of consistent, excellent service delivery to gain a loyal customer but such gain could be lost after a few minutes of carelessness or any form of staff misconduct. In fact, according to Hsieh Tony, customer service need not be a department, rather it should be the entire organisation itself.

In Nigeria, as a developing nation, the ideology of customer service and customer satisfaction has posed a great challenge to the service sector and our industry is not an exception to this challenge. When you consider competing factors that drive the industry, the financial input, competition among local and global brands, and the huge challenge for sustained growth, you will agree with me that customer service is KEY and should not be taken with levity or trivialized.

Customer care service simply means attending to a customer in such a way that leaves the customer with the feeling that he or she has gotten real good value for money paid. When you can say confidently, "Satisfaction guaranteed or your money back," and indeed the customer comes back for a repeat business despite the availability of alternatives, then you can ascertain that you've got good customer service.

Customer care is the act of taking care of the customer's needs by providing and delivering professional, helpful, high-quality service and assistance before, during and after the customer's requirements are met. This is indeed applicable to the aviation industry as service delivery starts from the time of meeting the travel consultant, to arranging the flights, to landing back at the airport. The service quality and delivery among the players in the chain have brought a lot of dissatisfaction to customers resulting into several operational shortcomings that have affected the image of the airline industry at large.

Speaking from personal experience and studies carried out by aviation researchers and business travellers, one could deduce that customers in the aviation industry mostly complain about issues like communication challenges such as poor feed-back, failure to act on customer's concerns, wrong use of language, flight delays and cancellations without prior notification, general lack of ethics and disrespectful behavior by workers. Others include, payment of unplanned expenses after payment of due tariff due to unbundled services and flight disruptions.

You can imagine the shiver that would run through one's spine when one gets to see not-so- friendly looking armed security agents parading the airport with their ammunitions hung all over. Such is the experience in aviation industries across the continent because of safety and security issues. All these, summed up, have caused a lot of irritation to customers. Customer retention is KEY. In the real sense of it, customers should be treated as kings.

Literally, when customer satisfaction is ensured, it would eventually result in cutting costs without cutting corners. This is accentuated by the fact that maintaining an old customer is less expensive than getting a new customer. An old customer would recommend the agent and or airline to friends, associates and family members. An unsatisfied customer (would have his or her own sphere of influence also) and such customers are discharged to destroy our business. Evidently, many airlines on record have shown that they went down the drain and into obscurity due to poor customer service.

## 1. WHO ARE THE CUSTOMERS?

By the way, taking a general look at who a customer really is, the business dictionary defines a customer as a party that receives or consumes products (goods or services) and has the ability to choose between different products and suppliers. Also, in sales, commerce and industry, a customer is the recipient of a good, service product and idea obtained from a seller or vendor through a financial transaction involving some exchange of valuable consideration.

This is applicable to the airline industry where "the commercial pay load." include the passenger, freight/cargo, mail, human remains, etc. As I have said earlier, the customer is key to the survival and success of any business. Of all these, passengers are the only ones who have feelings and the only ones that can either complain / condemn the quality of service rendered or commend the service rendered. They are the only ones who could have active engagement with the brand.

Passengers among the various categories of customers are the most desirous of care. It will be safe to say that customer care begins right at the time of meeting the travel agent up till landing back to the airport.

Indeed, the importance of being strategic and proactive in customer care management in aviation should not be ignored, especially when considered in light of dynamic realities of modern economic development and cost implications of losing the main source of income. The ripple-effects and the dire consequences that could result from cutting corners in this regard cannot be exaggerated.

Proper attention to customers' preferences as well as well engineered processes are essential to getting a satisfied customer base and enhancing an agency's/airline reputation.

a. **Passengers:** These are a set of customers that require the biggest care before, during and even after a flight. A passenger relies on the travel consultant for almost everything from buying a ticket, to check-in, security screenings, baggage loading and offloading, on flight and after flight services, etc. Caring for passengers has posed a great challenge instead of a great opportunity in the face of growing competition amongst airlines in Nigeria. Advancements in information technology systems are expected to improve the services of travel and make passenger boarding a lot easier safer and faster. Reports however, show mixed feelings when evaluating quality of services provided by travel management companies and even the airlines as one in about every thirty customers gets satisfied and seeks a repeat service. Reports of missed or delayed flights are fast becoming too rampant as if it is the norm in the Nigerian aviation space, with thousands of frustrated customers sometimes sharing their experiences on social media. Namukasa, in a report published in 2013, clearly asserts that excellent passenger satisfaction is one of the greatest assets for the aviation businesses in today's competitive environment. Therefore, for the airlines in Nigeria to survive and have a competitive edge as well as stand a global chance, the airline passengers who are the only set of customers that have feelings and initiatives, must be well catered for and be the central focus.

b. **Cargo:** This is another major source of income for an airline. air cargo/air freight refers to goods or commodity to be carried by air. Some airlines are freighters only meaning they strictly air lift cargoes and no passengers. Even though cargoes have no feelings and initiative, there should be care to avoid damages to properties which will adversely affect the image of the firm. Larger cargo airlines tend to use new or recently built aircrafts to carry their freight. However, many still utilize older aircrafts, fleets (not suited for passenger service), like the Boeing 707, Boeing 727, Douglas DC-8, DC-10, MD-11, Airbus A300, and the Ilyushin Il-76.

c. **Human Remains:** This refers to cargo of dead humans. It is the most expensive cargo rate of airlines. It is almost ten times the normal tariff rate for living passengers. This is informed by the delicate nature of carriage. No delays, no cancellations, no disruptions are expected to avoid decomposition and all scheduled burial plans. The dead cargo has no form of feeling and it would seem as if no special care is needed because the corpse cannot complain about poor handling. Unfortunately, such customers are rare as most people return their sick loved ones home before their demise.

When I talk about customer care service, it is a very crucial factor in the operation of aviation organisations as competition within the industry continues to grow. As I have stated earlier, the first point of contact are with the travel agents. Passengers require the greatest care and they totally depend and rely on the travel consultant or travel agent for guidance on their trip. Hence, a high level of efficiency is required from the travel agent.

The customer, after encountering the travel agent, goes to the airport. The aura of the airport and the ambience which can be seen and felt should provide customers with much relief and a sense of safety. Many needless processes can make the journey of a customer tedious and cumbersome. The many check points for example are a disincentive to travelling. In order to make the process of a passenger trying to navigate the airport terminals seamless, there is need for the availability of an efficient Flight Information Display System (FIDS) and signages that will perfectly ensure that passengers' expectations on easy navigation through the terminal zones are met. There is need for signages in English as well as local or other foreign languages in addition to pictograms throughout the airport for ease of movement.

Another area of concern is pilferage and broached baggage. I believe we have a lot to learn from Malaysia. According to a 2010 publication by the *Runway to Success*, Malaysian Airports have over the years come out with a few initiatives such as the establishment of a task force, working in close cooperation with both the police and airline security, installation of additional CCTVs at the baggage handling system conveyor belts, constant spot checks on baggage handlers, increase in manpower to guard passengers' baggage and increase in patrolling frequency. The initiatives have brought about improved service delivery since 2002, where reported pilferage cases are far below the global average of 80 bags per 100,000 passengers. It was much lower than the global average and the number of incidents continues to decrease on a downward trend. Safety is paramount to everyone and so much more to airline customers. Knowing that a lot of people parade the airport, it is quite essential that authentic safety schemes be put in place to reduce risks and threat to life. Ensuring safety at the airport should be geared towards providing passengers with a safe and seamless experience.

To make passengers' safety possible, it is the responsibility of the airport management to work closely with the appropriate airport community. Passengers' expectations of airport security are related to waiting time required for security check, the professionalism of the security staff, and the ability of the security process to make them feel safe. In addition, while on board, cabin crew who are actually trained safety officers are posted to ensure that passengers are comfortable on board even amid threatening situations. And after the flight on returning to the airport, excellent customer service is required from the airport ground management staff.

From my experience of the Nigerian setting, the reverse could be the case as passengers, sometimes after the very long trip, are made to go through undue long processes of checking and waiting.

Passengers' bags are sometimes handled without care, and sometimes customers' baggage and luggage arrive broached, wet/ soaked and damaged. Even, due to uncomfortable service while on board, there have been instances of passengers going back home feeling sick and having to spend quite some time in recovering. Harassment of customers by airport attendants is not uncommon. The heart desire of every airport management should be to surpass customers' expectations. It has been found out that often times, customers' perception of quality service is based on their expectations; these expectations are sometimes met with disappointment. When all these are considered, we can conclude that there is evidence of cutting corners. The use of technology does not mean the eradication of manpower, there should be manpower behind the technology for the purpose discretion. Hence, technologies are for the minimization of human errors and reinforcement of manpower; so in the end, no customer will blame gadgets and machines for failure.

## 2. CUSTOMER SERVICE BENCHMARKING PROGRAMME

Several customer service-benchmarking programmes have been established to systematically measure the customer satisfaction at the airport. The benchmarking programmes will measure the actual airport performance against desirable standard of customer service. All these programmes will provide key data points to the airport management so they can further understand the strengths and weaknesses of airport facilities and services and to identify the areas of improvement. In a way, it will provide the airport management with the mechanism to monitor and manage all other service providers at the airport such as those engaged in gate management, baggage handling, concessions, parking, and security checkpoints. There are instruments that have been designed and deployed for information gathering at the airports.

Airport Service Quality (ASQ) Survey is the Airport Council International (ACI) comprehensive initiative to improve the quality of service experienced by passengers with participation of over 200 airports in more than 50 countries. All airports use the same questionnaires and follow the same methodology to identify best practice and to measure their own performance precisely.

SKYTRAX Airport Star Rating is a programme that evaluates standards of frontline Product and Service quality for airports worldwide. The programme applies an evaluation system to assess the quality standards across each airport's operations to ensure that all airport quality rating is conducted in a standardized and consistent manner. The methodology is to evaluate the actualquality of service delivered.

## 3. DETERMINANTS OF CUSTOMER SATISFACTION

By putting in perspective the place of the customer in the airline industry, knowing that he or she is a crucial determinant of the growth of any business organization, it is important to consider if the quality of the services rendered can give the customer satisfaction in the truest sense. As asserted by Groth and Dye in their 1999 discourse on customer service, "A service (contemplated and expected) differs from the perceptions of quality of service received. Parasuraman, Zeithaml, and Berry who wrote in 1985 and 1988 respectively, proposed five dimensions that could be used to measure customer satisfaction. These can be applicable to the aviation industry as well.

These dimensions are:
- Tangibles
- Reliability
- Responsiveness
- Assurance and
- Empathy

Therefore, failure to ensure that customers have a quality, tangible service, will result in losing the customers and sourcing for new ones. This is always more expensive. Instead of cutting cost, cost is increased.

Apart from care of the customers, airline operators need to do more in terms of treatment of their staff. If the personnel are not properly taken care of in terms of benefits due to them and incentives, they could pass on their aggression to innocent customers. The end product then would be poor customer service.

At the very heart of improving the quality of service rendered in the airport is the introduction of technology. Life really becomes easy with properly utilized technology and this ensures cutting costs without cutting corners in the aviation industry as well as in other sectors.

The introduction of technology, though expensive but highly yielding, will (in the long run) reduce undue processes and the unnecessary stress associated with air travel.

This follows that the cabin crew and every other player and contributor in the aviation industry need the required training and attitude to render specialized and professional services to their customers. A win for the customers would be a win for the business and a win for the staff.

# CHAPTER TEN

# ACCOUNTING:
## Cost Reduction vs. Compromise

Accounting is the process of taking stock of the assets and liabilities of a business in comparison with its expenses and revenues. This process is very important for players within the aviation industry in order to ascertain growth or decline of the respective firms. Accounting is a must for any businesses that is serious about making profit. Although in the aviation industry it is expected that safety should be considered as first in the order of priority. The need to ensure safety and continued existence of the company must remain paramount because all airline operators need to manage inherent costs of operations to remain afloat. Yet, there is always the need to identify where the thin line between strategies targeted at cost reduction tend to cross over to the compromise side, which would invariably affect safety. Cost reduction within the aviation industry is a strategy adopted to reduce costs, eliminate unwarranted expenses and improve profits.

It usually affects all decisions pertaining to the operations of the airline. However, when cost reduction is carried out without necessary care, due diligence and consideration of compliance risks, it tends to cross the thin line into compromise. In the Nigerian aviation industry, the Nigerian Civil Aviation Authority (NCAA) is saddled with the responsibility of ensuring that compromise does not take the upper hand, yet the administrative deficiencies of the industry has tilted the fulcrum more in favour of compromise because of insufficient attention by the regulatory bodies.

While fingers are regularly being pointed at the regulator on safety compromises, I would want to state categorically that safety is a major responsibility of the operator in that there are several coordinated activities that ought to give rise to safety and efficiency beyond the eyes of the regulator. The operator that self regulates is the operator not only for today but tomorrow and beyond.

We will therefore examine safety responsibilities from various perspectives: *Human capital, training & skill acquisition, expatriates and transfer of technology, MRO facility, aircraft acquisition & leasing and authourised Airline Training Organisations (ATOs)*

## 1. SAFETY AND HUMAN CAPITAL

Regardless of investments made in technology and automation deployed in the operations of airports, airlines, and even runways, the critical role of the human capital needed to ensure proper use of these technologies and safety cannot be underestimated. The operations of the best technological device is subject to the capacity, skill, whims and caprices of the user, bringing to mind the saying, *"garbage in, garbage out"*. Hence, the need to ensure that a high premium is paid on getting workers who are satisfied, competent and contented, as anything short of this has been seen to have disastrous ends when high levels of compromise set in.

In Nigeria, employers tend to capitalize on the high unemployment rate leading to a bloated labour market and the availability of many options. Although they often recruit people with the right competences, adequate compensation is never paid because they want to cut operational costs. This hardly ever ends well.

We've had incidences of pilots who do not log-in their flight crew schedules or snag reports, and consequently tend to make more trips in order to make more money. Sometimes the schedule officers are compromised to get more flying hours to the detriment of the crew's rest time.

Bellview Airlines Flight 210 that crashed on 22nd October, 2005 at Lisa-Igbore village in Ogun State was largely rumoured to be linked to such an unfortunate scenario. The obviously fatigued pilot could not think clearly as the iron bird nose-dived into mother earth.

The investigation was hampered by lack of physical evidence on the crash site which was caused by the aircraft's high speed impact and after crash lootings. The flight data recorder (FDR) and cockpit voice recorder (CVR) were not recovered and forensic analysis on the pilots could not be conducted. As such, the investigation was inconclusive according to the Accidents Investigation Bureau (AIB). This draws attention to the non-compliance of log book documentation and monitoring by the airline operator, as pilots tend to see themselves as kings of the air.

Often times, sufficient workforce per average number of aircraft in the operation of an airline is not engaged, such that the few workers become overworked and overburdened with the work of many, making focus very difficult. In many cases, workers are multitasked by asking them to handle many port folios. We tend to have employees that are constantly struggling to meet up with the ever-increasing customer satisfaction demands of the organization.

These compromises undermine the safety focus and are allowed to continue because corrupt regulators turn a blind eye to the situation. While seeking to control and cut costs, no airline operator should compromise on staff quality & quantity, commensurate remuneration and general welfare and work conditions of employees.

## 2. TRAINING

Airline operators are sometimes guilty of allowing training and retraining of their workforce take the back seat, not necessarily as a cost reduction strategy but because of its place on the priority list. Profit optimisation within a set time frame tends to be prioritized over and above safety of the travelling public. But one is tempted to lean on this side of the coin as no proper structure and sufficient aviation education is presently available (until recently) in Nigeria. Babcock University recently introduced MBA Programme in Airline Studies.

Prior to this, airlines had to send their employees abroad (at huge forex costs) if they wanted them to be up-to-date with the dynamic global aviation industry. In a bid to manage costs, staff training and retraining which should be done periodically is down played and held sparingly may be once in a year if at all. This is indeed a ticking time bomb waiting to explode. The consequence of this obvious error of omission and commission is that the workforce is not mentally equipped to match the challenges of the ever dynamic technological and artificial intelligence (AI) presently and rapidly changing global trade, aviation in particular.

Nigerian College of Aviation Technology (NCAT), Zaria, established for training the crew (cockpit & cabin), engineers and operation workers has been dilapidated with the equipment far from being up-to-date.

It is against this backdrop and the need to prioritize training that the Minister of State for Aviation, Senator Hadi Sirika at a seminar titled, *"The Nigerian Aviation Education Infrastructure – Challenges and*

*Potential,"* sought to emphasize the need to define our aviation education policies for Approved Training Organizations (ATOs) and various higher educational bodies (polytechnics, universities and others). The minister realized the need for Nigerian colleges, universities and other approved aviation training institutions to define the policy and strategy that would allow for the training of staff and even graduate students who will join the global industry in the future, to learn about safety, security and customer service in a satisfactory manner.

## 3. EXPATRIATES AND TRANSFER OF TECHNOLOGY

Due to the shortage of highly skilled technical personnel in the aviation industry, Nigerian airline operators end up paying for expatriates who would receive double the remuneration of indigenous alternatives. The practice is that most of the expatriate pilots and engineers would work with these Nigerian airlines for six months and enjoy six months holiday. The airlines are usually shortchanged in terms of service availability, yet the additional cost of first-class tickets for their movements must be billed into the running costs attributed to their welfare package.

In order to save costs, there is a tendency for operators to only employ few of such expatriates, and keep less qualified pilots as copilots who are expected to watch, learn and train under the expatriates. These co-pilots are allowed to fly the planes in times of emergencies. This practice, unfortunately, sometimes goes unnoticed; or it could be that the compliance officers and regulatory bodies turn a blind eye to these compromises made all in a bid to reduce cost attributable to recruiting pilots with sufficient hours. There is no local content law that makes it mandatory for all foreign airlines operating into Nigeria to have a Nigerian pilot and cabin crew on its personnel data. A local content law would therefore go a long way in creating new jobs for Nigerian professionals and also cutting down some of the capital flights linked to the foreign experts. If the Nigerian aviation workforce is trained to adequately meet the needs of the aviation industry in line with global best practices, they could become expatriates themselves and begin to provide such services to other nations. This will be made possible by increased investments in aviation education, the enabling environment, and the modern aviation infrastructure that students, teachers, instructors and professors would be able to access in their training institutions. The economic multiplier effect of having well trained, globally respected pilots and engineers within and outside the country would be awesome in the long run for the nation as home repatriation of funds would benefit the Nigerian economy.

## 4. MAINTENANCE, REPAIR & OVERHAUL (MRO) FACILITY

One of the most indispensable cost elements in the airline industry is the compulsory maintenance of aircrafts. This is indeed more challenging for airline businesses in Nigeria because the aircrafts must be ferried overseas for maintenance. This process usually gulps huge sums of money, as costs attributable to aviation fuel, landing charges, parking charges must be taken care of, in addition to the checks (C-D) maintenance itself. Also, the payment of the pilots and engineers that would be involved in ferrying the aircraft, and the inclusion of costs that would cover payments for the inspectors to the maintenance facilities from the Nigerian Civil Aviation Authority (NCAA) must be provided for.

The practice is that many airlines tend to ensure that the regular A-checks and B-checks are done routinely, while the C-checks are delayed. The downside of this action is the long-run effect on safety. Compromises begin at this stage and the tendency for air crashes to occur becomes more inevitable. In some instances, the NCAA officers expected to ensure compliance would feign ignorance largely because they have been compromised through corruption to allow for delays in compliance with checks. Even though this practice is meant to reduce the operational costs for the airline operators in the short-run, the long-run cost, like a rat that sees itself as an expert in eating tasty meals placed on a trap, it hardly ever ends well.

Interestingly and positively too, the NCAA has granted an approval to Aero Contractors Airline to conduct IC"- checks on certain Boeing aircraft series at its Aircraft Maintenance Organisation (AMO) workshop in Ikeja, Lagos. This approval is the first given to any airline and would include availability to do C-checks for Boeing 737-300; 400; 500; 600; 700 and 800 series aircrafts. It would allow for a comprehensive eighteen months maintenance repairs on aircrafts. Once this becomes operational, it would lead to at least 50 percent cost reduction in business operations of the Nigerian airline players.

One may begin to worry however, that *will compromise in the maintenance process not repeat itself again? Will the regulators also ensure constant monitoring of this Aero"s AMO workshop & practices to forestall air calamities in the near future?* These unanswered questions a-la-Nigerian factor must be carefully addressed.

## 5. AIRCRAFT ACQUISITION & LEASING

Leasing of aircrafts is an aircraft acquisition option alternative among others. We are used to assuming that if an airline paints an aircraft using its livery and operates it, it must also own it. This is far from the reality. The incredible financial burden of procuring a brand-new aircraft is so significant that virtually all airlines decide to lease at least some of their aircraft fleet. Also, the trend towards aircraft leasing has become very popular due to volatile competitive rivalries, and the frequent changing nature of the business in aviation. Competition and change restrain both the financial capacity of airlines and their ability to raise debt. Therefore, in recent years most airlines have been relying on leasing aircrafts rather than buying as a way of doing business and as an alternative to the huge up front capital that is required when purchasing new or used aircraft.

Aircraft lease could be wet, dry and/or damp. A dry lease is the case in which a commercial airline takes aircraft from the leasing company for a set period of time. In most cases, the aircraft remains on the livery of the leasing company and the airline operates it using its own crew. It is the most common type of leasing. Wet leasing engages the Aircraft, Crew, Maintenance, Insurance (ACMI) from the leasor airline and changes the aircraft livery to its own because more often than not, it serves as ad-hoc when an airline introduces additional aircraft to fill the gap during a long time maintenance period. A typical experience was when the global 787 fleet became grounded due to their trent engine issues. These are usually short term and total contract values are much less than those of dry leases. Damp leases are when the lessor provides the aircraft, flight crew, and maintenance, while the leasee provides the cabin crew.

I have also observed other deals known as "Sale and Lease back." This is a financial transaction in which an airline sells its aircraft to another aircraft leasing company and then leases it back for the long term; therefore, the airline continues to be able to use the aircraft but no longer owns it. The most common reason for such transactions is to free up capital and obtain cash. Agreements as such happen quite regularly and historically, it is more among financially troubled carriers, as cash becomes more valuable for their short-term survival. According to the International Council on Clean Transportation (ICCT), the need to expand fleet sizes to accommodate the growth in air passengers has led to an increase of aircraft leasing companies and financial instruments that aim to provide debt financing. However, this option is not economically viable and is incompatible with the aviation business environment in Nigeria. Nigerians lack technical expertise and understanding of the intricacies surrounding leasing and insurance arrangements. It costs Nigerian airlines more to lease their aircraft and also the insurance premium for aircraft operating in Nigeria is relatively very high.

It has been observed by experts and confirmed by the author that, the conditions given to Nigerian airlines considering leasing of aircrafts are too stringent, hence it seems more cost- effective for an outright purchase of aircraft instead. Many reasons or excuses are given for this reluctance by these potential leasors with some stating the unsafe Nigerian business environment as the major reason. Others dwell on the unsupportive nature of government and the sanctity of its laws. As such, the resultant capital flight is inevitable because our airline operators – without the option of leasing – would have to buy off these aircrafts to remain in business. The situation is more pathetic when one considers the fact that, there is no protection rendered from the regulators or negotiations made in favour of the airline operators hence these firms are left as orphans to deal with the costs which stare them in the face. However, if efforts are put in place to ensure that Nigeria gets its own aircraft leasing company like General Electric Commercial Aviation Services (GECAS), the aviation finance arm of General Electric (GE), the country and the industry would save costs upwards of $500 million in cost of leasing and compromises would be brought to the barest minimum.

## 6. OTHERS CHALLENGES

Airline operators have lamented the poor state of the airport terminals and runways of some of the airports in the country, as well as the non-existence of navigational aids required to support flight operations after 6pm. Many of these airline operators tend to invest some of their organization's finances in providing temporary help, so as to meet customer expectations and timelines. For example, at the aviation round table conference (2018) held at the Golfview Suites & Conference Centre, Ikeja GRA, Allen Onyema, the CEO of Air Peace, stated that his company provided a generating set for the Owerri International Airport to power the lights for the runway. As a result of this, the company aircrafts have been able to meet scheduled night landing flights. This exogenous cost would obviously affect the firm's cost reduction strategy as it is totally outside its direct cost of operations. There was another incident at Ibadan local airport in 2019 when an airline, after take-off from Abuja on schedule and was close to landing, heard that the airport had been closed because night landing facilities had been shut down. This was without prior notice. According to the report, the normal airport time for the day had elapsed and the airport officials had shut down the airport. The airline had to put a call through to the airport authority in Ibadan, and urge them to put on the airport facilities for them promising to bear the cost. This was an exogenous cost to the airline.

Unfortunately, these sorts of gestures, howbeit commendable, invariably gives rise to sympathetic disposition of the regulatory apparatus within the state, and so when such an airline does not meet certain compliance requirements, it is literally waived with a lot of consideration for the "perceived earlier contribution" which tends to cover their negligence.

## THE REGULATOR – LONG RUN COMPROMISE EFFECT

The Nigerian Civil Aviation Authority is the umbrella body saddled with the onerous task of regulating the aviation sector in the country. As a result, the authority must be procedurally and technically competent to handle any or all of the issues in the industry. It is expected to ensure that the aviation industry balances appropriately on the tripod stand of Safety, Speed and Accuracy with integrity and high regulations. It is expected to promote peace and good working relationships among the airline operators as well as confirm the fitness of facilities at the airports before use. Yet, saddled with these humongous responsibilities, the regulator has not been able to successful carry out its functions successfully, leading to many colossal losses.

A clear example is the case of a domestic flight which carried some dignitaries, including serving ministers, nearly crashing just because weather reports were not taken before the aircraft took off. This is a compliance requirement to ensure that the weather is good and provides safety for sojourners from their point of origin to their destination, yet it is usually taken for granted and sometimes ignored.

Another misnomer is when airlines have to pay for travels and allowances to be undertaken by NCAA regulators on their way to certify an aircraft. This makes it difficult if not impossible for such airlines to be regulated appropriately without prejudice or bias on matters of safety as he who pays the piper dictates the tune. The aircraft type being utilized by many of the airline operators (which is the Boeing 737) is designed more as regional aircrafts to cover durations up to six hours. Regrettably this is the aircraft being used for domestic operations in Nigerian with 45min / 1 hour sector flight durations. This creates huge costs for fueling versus deepening revenue levels. Even at full capacity and at the prevailing tariff, breakeven point will remain a huge challenge. For example, when a 737 aircraft is loaded with about twenty passengers on a flight to Abuja at a cost of 35,000 naira, and the aviation fuel on a return flight costs over half a million naira, the revenue generated will be a paltry N700,000.00 which does not even cover aviation fuel, not to talk of other ancillary expenses required for a round trip. B737 at full capacity cannot also carry up to a ton of cargo hence there's no cost complement in the cargo hold either.

The regulators have not been able to insist that airline operators deploy only aircrafts that are commercially and economically viable for the available sectors in Nigeria. Unfortunately, most airlines mostly fly aircrafts they can get not aircrafts needed. The constant trend of purchasing modern airplanes has been bleeding the finances of many airline operators. To worsen this trend, most pilots tend to seek their type ratings with Boeing since other manufacturers such as Airbus are more expensive.

Aside this discourse on aircraft types, unchecked activities of union officials of the Nigerian Civil Aviation Authority have also made it a difficult for the management of the Authority to checkmate officials that have been known to compromise on safety related issues. It is indeed preposterous that some of these union officials are uninformed, as evidenced in their display of ignorance by promoting misinformation and falsehood about events in the industry, all in a bid to portray those who are providing jobs for teeming Nigerians and foreigners alike in bad light. They do all these in the name of unionism. They selfishly do this to strengthen their arguments, laced with half-truths and outright lies to gain public sympathy for their wrong actions which are targeted at disrupting the operations of the airlines and the airport terminals. They operate like bullies.

A clear example as stated in the report of Hadejia (2018) is given below: "For instance, it is shocking, embarrassing and indeed laughable that the Secretary General of the National Union of Air Transport Employees, Olayinka Abioye, would step out at a recent stakeholder's forum organized by the Nigerian Airspace Management Agency in Lagos to say that Dana Air has surreptitiously brought in a foreign airline, Asky, to operate domestic flights in Nigeria, when in actual fact, the plane is in on wet-lease to Dana and NCAA approved it. Anybody worth its salt in the aviation industry should know that airlines are protected by law to go on either wet-lease or dry lease of aircrafts from other airlines. This clearly shows the level of ignorance and illiteracy among the aviation union leaders who claim to be fighting for the rights of workers. It is like the blind leading the eyed."

There is hardly any critical investor in the aviation industry today that has not tasted the bitter pill of the unions' unruliness and recalcitrance. Airlines such as Arik Air, Aero Contractors, Dana, Landover and others have lost millions of dollars to the unions' brigandage in the name of picketing. Even the Bi-Courtney Aviation Services Limited, operators of the internationally acclaimed Murtala Muhammed Airport Terminal Two (MMA2), has also tasted this bitter pill, disguised as reoccurring threats of the unions.

It is instructive to note therefore that the inability of the regulators of the Nigerian aviation industry to curtail the excesses of some of its union employees has brought a lot of non-compliant attitudes, which have become major risk factors. This in turn has given rise to many compromising behaviours. This has been capitalized upon by the airline operators, with manipulations targeted at cutting costs, invariably leading to a wipe out of the main tenets of the aviation industry: Safety, Security, Speed and Accuracy. The result seems good in the short run, as revenue generated is celebrated while the long-run effect is known to the wise even before the worst comes.

# CHAPTER ELEVEN

# PROFIT MAXIMIZATION:
## Ethics and Profit

As I have noted earlier, the desire of every business enterprise is maximization of profit. Yet, the ability of every business to maximize profit without cutting corners, and without compromising any moral or ethical standards is of utmost importance.

Ethics x-rays the moral issues that can arise in any business. As long as we are dealing with human beings who trust us with their lives and properties, the question of right and wrong, the question of fairness, will always arise.

The philosophy of every business is reflected through its business ethics. For example, an airline desiring to maximize shareholders wealth and profits will naturally tend to ignore and negate (even if not deliberately) the position of trust that the customers have placed on it. Normative dimension of business ethics, which attempts to underscore business behaviour, magnitude and quality of business practices of the enterprise itself, reflects on the interaction of profit maximizing. However, the descriptive dimension reveals how government uses laws and regulations to point at business behaviours of players that underlie beyond government control.

In Nigeria, airline business may look appealing for investment, especially because the country is blessed with the biggest domestic aviation market on the continent, yet, the huge opportunity in this market has not been properly harnessed for the benefit of the country.

Even though Nigerian airlines have been operating for years, they have not been able to hack the secret of successful airline business operations; and it may remain elusive if the focus is on cutting corners rather than cutting costs.

Nigerian airline businesses are mostly unprofitable due to a large number of reasons which can be attributed to multiple factors, and as such the desire to make profits has caused many players to discount ethical practices, at the detriment of life, property and existence of the companies.

## THE ETHICAL DILEMMA

Duty theories in ethical thoughts are based on the idea of doing the right thing even if it comes with a cost. Consequentialist ethical theories describe ethical actions as those that yield positive results. The most influential consequentialist theory is utilitarianism, which stresses "the greatest benefit for the greatest number." Utilitarianism is highly influential in ethical thoughts as it remains the foundation upon which the business ethos of customer service and utility maximization was formed. Pragmatist ethics on the other hand, though less prominent, stresses the value of outcome above principles and accepts that the same actions can be considered ethical or unethical in different circumstances. Pragmatist ethics influences the basic business ethos of self-interest and doing well by meeting the consumer's demands. There is widespread lack of commitment to ethical behaviour, and little or no concern for excellence and self-reliance in Nigeria and in Nigerian organisations.

Akinyemi, in his submission on ethics published in 2002, noted that one of the greatest social and economic problems in Nigeria and indeed Africa, which must be tackled, is that of breakdown in morals, work ethics, discipline, social responsibility and general civility among its citizens. Similarly, Douglas Adams in his discourse on the provision of service published in 1987, also noted that "to give real service, you must add something which cannot be bought or measured with money, and that is sincerity and integrity."

These ingredients are lacking in the Nigerian business environment. On the contrary, there is executive recklessness, corporate impunity, corruption and lack of adherence to corporate governance. Researchers and authors Bruce Mckern, Philip Meza, Ekinadese Osayande and Lyn Denend, in their research paper published in 2010, observed that for decades, Nigeria had grappled with religious and ethnic unrest as well as highly unequal allocation of resources, and doubted if the momentum of recent reforms could be sustained to create a business environment that would make for global competition and investment. Therefore, understanding the customer spread of aviation industry globally should underpin every business decision not profit maximization. It is unfortunate that ours is a society where pecuniary concerns override integrity and this has permeated every facet, thus inflating the stake on integrity to the extent that, it is hardly considered during business dealings as, the end seems to justify the means.

## 1. THE AVIATION BUSINESS ENVIRONMENT

The Aviation business environment in Nigeria is saddled with a lot of challenges which have been seen to make the saying "desperate times call for desperate measures" true. Some of these challenges are seen to make profit lines thin out; the response of some airlines to these sometimes-daunting challenges is to toss ethics in the bin in the desperation to make profit.

a.  **Aircraft Maintenance:** Aircraft maintenance is an expensive venture. Although the Class A and B checks are run on aircrafts within Nigeria, the Class C checks are carried out only abroad.

This Overseas Aircraft Maintenance (OAM) is very expensive for the airlines coupled with the exchange rate fluctuations. I have seen instances of faults that should have been discovered during Class A and B checks, discovered during the Class C overseas checks. Do you know what that says about the quality of the A and B checks?

b. **Exchange Rate:** A glaring issue affecting the profit position of airlines within the country lies in the exchange rate variance between the Nigerian naira and foreign currencies particularly the dollar. While Nigerian airlines earn their revenues in local currency, aircraft acquisition (purchase/lease), insurance and maintenance costs are paid in foreign currency which leads to huge losses when converted. This has led to the shutdown of many airlines in the past and is still plaguing present operators.

c. **High Cost of Aviation Fuel:** The aviation fuel known as Jet A1 (ATK) is usually not readily available and when it is, it comes relatively too expensive. Airplanes have been seen waiting endlessly at the tarmac to be refueled while supplies coming in trucks would have travelled long distances before arrival with the possibility of fuel contamination. This, in many instances, results in delayed flights and some incidences through water in fuel contamination. Civilized economies (including Nigeria in the past) deploy Fuel Hydrants which convey fuel directly from the depot to the tarmac. Regrettably the Nigeria hydrant has been abandoned and left un-served, but left to rot away over the years, leaving road haulage as an alternative in a bid to cut costs. But in essence, not using hydrants for fuel supply is cutting corners. This is absurd in an oil rich country such as Nigeria as this process also increases fuel costs considering the addition of haulage charges per liter of fuel.

d. **Government's Indifference:** The government has been indifferent to the plight of airline operators for a long time. While airline businesses are struggling to make progress and deliver the much-needed service to the public, government agencies have ignored their many demands to help improve airline businesses in Nigeria. Some airport costs absorbed by the airlines have been enumerated earlier and many more like inefficient runway lightings, neglect of routine maintenance of runways, occasional loss of communication between points, etc. This is simply because the airport and air space service providers are a government monopoly and could not care less when some of these cost burdens are directly or indirectly borne by the airlines. There seems to be a conspiracy of silence among government parastatals expected to make the running of the airlines smooth and seamless, as airline operators are left to deal with the issues with their own funds, thereby further reducing their own available funds for business operations. The agencies also struggle to survive commercially and wouldn't care less. For example, FAAN has no current policy of giving land at little or no cost to attract investments in tooling hangar and manpower training. This would have gone a long way in resolving some teething problems, which operators have to deal with routinely. The Assets Management Corporation of Nigeria (AMCON) too cannot absolve itself completely from the travails of the airlines they took over. The corporation has been involved in the renegotiation and rescheduling of many loans owed by some airlines to the banks and to the federal government to the detriment of running efficient airlines. Its recommendation on how to progress with the airlines under them is not agreeable to the aviation ministry, thus suggesting a dysfunction in government.

A mind boggling question remains: How can AMCON allow a privately owned airline to have a debt portfolio of up to N268billion collected from six different banks as at 2014? Although, AMCON was aware of this peculiar anomaly, it still allowed the airline access to the federal government aviation intervention funds. With these airlines having to service such huge debt profile, clearly the issue of profitability at all cost to remain afloat is being encouraged not just by AMCON but also by some banks. This is a huge part of the industry's travails.

e. **Dearth in Infrastructure:** The deficit in infrastructure also poses a challenge. It is estimated that losses incurred owing to power outages amount to 10% of sales and production. Most Nigerian airports are not fully equipped with the requirements as stipulated by the International Air Transport Association (IATA) to manage airlines. The control towers have outdated equipment, the runways are more of death traps with pot holes, uneven surfaces and lack of lighting tracks and this continues to pose dangerous challenges for landing and taking off by airlines.

f. **Funds Diversion:** The aim of most operators in the industry is to make quick money while they have poor financial administration and poor corporate governance. They often selfishly divert airline funds into other ventures and strip the company. This scenario plagued many collapsed indigenous carriers such as Okada Air, Oriental Airlines, Chanchangi, Air Nigeria, Sosoliso, EAS and Bellview among others (see the table below):

## 2. LIST OF DEFUNCT COMMERCIAL AIRLINES IN NIGERIA

| S/ N | Airline | IATA | ICAO | Callsign | Commenced Operations | Ceased Operations | Outcome |
|------|---------|------|------|----------|----------------------|-------------------|---------|
| 1. | ADC Airline | | ADK | ADCO | 1984 | 2006 | |
| 2 | Aerocontract ors Company of Nigeria | NU; AJ | NIG | ACN | 1960 | 2002 | Renam ed/ merged to Aero Contrac |
| 3. | African International Airway | | | | 1971 | 1972 | |
| 4. | African Trans Air | | FTS | | 1992 | 1995 | |
| 5. | Afrijet Airlines | 6F | FRJ | AFRIJE T | 1998 | 2009 | |
| 6. | Afrimex | | | | 1994 | 2003 | |
| 7. | Air Atlantic Cargo | | ANI | | 1994 | 1999 | |
| 8. | Air Nigeria | VK | ANP | NIC ON FLI ERS | 2010 | 2012 | |
| 9. | Albarka Air | F4 | NBK | AL-AIR | 1999 | 2005 | |
| 1 0. | Al-Dawood Air | | LIE | AL- DAW OO D AIR | 2001 | 2005 | |
| 1 1. | Amako Air | | OBK | | 2002 | 2003 | |
| 1 2. | Amed Air | | OBI | | 1994 | 1996 | |
| 1 3. | Arax Airlines | QY | RXA | | 1977 | 1988 | |

| | | | | | | | |
|---|---|---|---|---|---|---|---|
| 1 4. | Associated Aviation | SCD | | ASSO CIA TED | 2006 | 2019 | |
| 1 5. | Axiom Air | | EAN | | 2009 | 2011 | |
| 1 6. | Barnax Air | | | | 1991 | 1992 | |
| 1 7 | Bellview Airlines | **B3** | BLV | BELL VIEW AIRLI NES | 1992 | 2010 | |
| 18. | Capital Airlines | | NCP | | 2003 | 2010 | |
| 19. | Central Airlines | | | | 1980 | 1982 | |
| 20. | Chanchangi Airlines | B5 | NCH | CHANGC HANGI | 1994 | 2012 | |
| 21. | Chrome Air Service | | CHO | Chrome Air | 1999 | 2006 | |
| 22. | Dasab Airlines | | DSQ | Dasab Air | 2001 | 2006 | |
| 23. | Earth Airlines | | ERX | | 2001 | 2004 | |
| 24. | EAS Airlines | O W | EX W | ECH OLI N E | 1993 | 2006 | Rebr ande d as Nico n |
| 25. | EAS Carg o Airli | | FY E | FLY ME | 2001 | 2007 | |

| | | | | | | | |
|------|-----------------------|-----|-------|----------------------|------|-------|---|
| 26. | First Nation Airways | | FRN | FIRST NATION | 2010 | 2018 | |
| 27. | Flash Airlines | | FS H | | 1985 | 1995 | |
| 28. | Freedom Air Service | | FFF | INTERFRE EDO | 1998 | 2005 | |
| 29. | Fresh Air | | FRR | Fresh Air | 1999 | 2006 | |
| 30. | GAS Air Nigeria | GR | NGS | | 1973 | 2000 | |
| 31. | Hamsal Air | 2H | M HL | | 2008 | 20009 | |
| 32. | Hamzair | | HMZ | Nigeria Int'l Air services | 1983 | 1983 | |
| 33. | Harco Air Service | | HCO | | 1992 | 1998 | |
| 34. | Hold-Trad | | | | 1991 | 2000 | |
| 35. | | | | | | | |
| 36. | IAT Cargo | | | Int'l Air Tours of | 1985 | 1987 | |
| 37. | IAT Carg o Airli nes | | VGO | Int'l Air Tours | | | |

| 38. | Interc ontin ental Airli | VS | VVV | | 1978 | 1990 | | | |
|---|---|---|---|---|---|---|---|---|---|
| 39. | IRS Airlines | IS | LV B | SILVERBIRD | 2002 | 2013 | | | |
| 40. | Kabo Air | Q N; K O; N2 ;N 9 | QNK | Kabo Air Travels | 1975 | 2016 | Started operations in 4/1981. AOC renewed by government 5/07. Suspended operations in 2016, remaining assets seized in 3/17 by tax authorities. | | |
| 41. | Man gal Airli nes | | NGL | | 2006 | 2008 | Rebranded as MaxAir (Nigeria) | | |
| 42. | Med- View Airline | M EV | VL | MED-VIEW | 2007 | 2019 | | | |
| 43. | Merchant Express Aviation | | MXX | MERCHANT | | Prior to 2000 | | | |
| 44. | Meridian Airlines | HL | M HL | | 2004 | 2008 | | | |
| 45. | Nicon Airways | OW | EX W | NICON AIRWAY | 2006 | 2007 | | | |
| 46. | Nigeria Airways | | WT | NGA | NIGERIA | 1971 | 2003 | | |
| 47. | Nigeria One | | | | | | 2013 | 2013 | Rebran ded as Nigeria n Eagle |
| 48. | Nigerian Eagle | VK | | VGN | | | 2009 | 2010 | Rebran ded as Air Nigeria |

| | | | | | | | |
|---|---|---|---|---|---|---|---|
| 49. | Nigerian Global Aviation | | NGI | | 2003 | 2003 | |
| 50. | Okada Air | 9H | OKJ | Okada Air | 1982 | 2002 | |
| 51. | Overnight Cargo Nigeria | | OCL | | 1992 | 1994 | |
| 52. | Pan African Airlines | PF | | | 1961 | 2000 | |
| 53. | Premium Air Shuttle | | EMI | | 1995 | 2006 | |
| 54. | Skypower Express Airways | NB | EAN | NIGERIA EXPRESS | 1985 | 2007 | |
| 55. | Slok Air International | SO | OKS | SLOK GAMBI A | 1996 | 2004 | Reforme d as Slok Air Gam bia Limit |
| 56. | Sosoliso Airlines | SO | OSL | SOSOLISO | 1994 | 2006 | |
| 57. | S p a c e Wo r l d International Airlines | | SPF | | 2002 | 2006 | |
| 58. | TAT Nigeria | | | | | | |
| 59. | Trans Sahara Air | | SJB | | 2001 | 2004 | |
| 60. | Trans-Air Services | | TSN | | 1992 | 1994 | |
| 61. | Triax Airlines | | TIX | | 1992 | 2000 | |
| 62. | UAS Cargo | SY | | United Air Services | 1985 | 1987 | Rebrand ed as EAS Carg o Airli nes |
| 63. | Virgin Nigeria | VK | VGN | | 2004 | 2009 | |

| 64. | Wings Aviation | | TWDD | TRADE W INGS | 2001 | 2012 | Merged into JedAir |
|---|---|---|---|---|---|---|---|

Source: Wikipedia

## 3. ETHICAL ISSUES AND PROFIT EROSION – THE PRACTICE

Interestingly, although the aviation business environment is known to be a challenging space as it practically erodes the perceived profits of airlines, the players within the sector are so focused on satisfying investors by meeting targets, improving returns on investment, as well as maximizing profits, while the welfare or honest concern for passengers/customers take the back seat.

a. **Profit Maximization at All Costs:** It doesn't matter whether you are a start-up or a multinational, every business is looking to grow its profits. Thus, profit maximization involves processes adopted or adapted by companies to determine the best output and price levels to achieve their goals. In this case, a firm achieves profit maximization when it reaches the stage of equilibrium. Hence, it has no need to change its level of output to maximize profit. However, if a business faces tough competition, sometimes the only way it can survive is to pay extra attention to revenues and costs and to adjust them accordingly.

The concept of profit maximization is a good thing for a company, the aviation industry inclusive, but it can be a bad thing for customers if the company starts to use cheaper products or decides to raise prices indiscriminately as a way to maximize profits. So, when it comes to profit maximization in business, according to McCormick (2017), there are two simple options open to you either to sell more or cut cost. Nevertheless, the 'profit maximization at all costs' syndrome which promotes substandard service delivery/product at higher costs while hiding the reality from customers, and at customers expense in order to cut corners, is unacceptable.

The desperation for profit maximization is largely because the airline companies are majorly one-man businesses with some small foreign partnerships. So, the norm is that the few small airline players lack financial muscle and so tend to cut corners to stay afloat, violating many ethical practices in the process. The bigger corporations owned by the multinationals are basically preoccupied with the business of customer satisfaction while making good profit while the small companies often lack such ethics. We can now appreciate what the good book says, "...for everyone to whom much is given, from him much will be required; and to whom much has been committed, of him they will ask the more" (Luke 12:48).

The airline operators require data analysis and business market demands tools, to be able to plan passenger schedules and frequencies. This tool helps to guide airlines in management decision-making for profit maximization. It includes a model for simulating how factors like revenue, demand, business behaviour, preferred class of travel, etc, connect. For instance, the trade-off in between business travelers and leisure travelers are dependent on the number of discounted seats offered for bookings. These are because, the business travelers are always ready to buy tickets either at discounted prices or full, while leisure travelers tend to buy only discounted fares.

Experience has shown that business travelers account for approximately 60% of most flights while leisure travelers account for the remaining 40% of the capacity.

An airline with good revenue management tool will decide on how many seats it will avail to every class of travel at differing tariffs.

**b. Investor Red Flags:** Many times, when an airline is known for unethical practices, passengers/customers desist from flying with them as the safety of their lives and property is not guaranteed. The airline begins to experience a high attrition rate from its crew and staff members and investors' confidence takes the back seat. This affects the growth or sustainability of the corporation. In some cases, if a serious ethical breach occurs, unions, activists, regulators and institutional investors step in and take action. This can present a costly, painful and risky turnaround challenge and it can become extremely difficult to save the credibility of the brand.

**c. Faulty Business Plans:** Some airline players in the aviation industry lack articulated, robust and fresh business plans. They simply copy and pasted old and sometimes untested business plans which might work in the short run but will fail in the long run. This has resulted in stunted growth in the sector. An aviation expert and former commandant at Murtala Muhammed Airport, Lagos, Group Captain John Ojikutu (Rtd), was credited for stating that most Nigerian airline operators are not grounded in commercial aviation. The business plan requirement as stated in the Nigerian Civil Aviation Regulation (NCAR), and to be processed by prospective airline operators for the approval of their Air Operator's Certificate (AOC) and/ or Air Operator's License (AOL), were usually copied from the airlines that existed before in Nigeria. These business plans have never reall y passed the sustainability test for the operation of airlines, yet are constantly recopied and accepted with no scrutiny by the regulators as to their workability. Also, it has been observed that these business plans tend to give temporary relief and tend to thrive in the short-run as proxies or partners in government agencies and ministries, while the legislature provide safe haven for debts owed on services provided to the airline practitioners by government operators. Favors that give room for government interventions to airline operators such as low interest rates; authorization of zero duties on aircraft spare parts; and concessional low rate on foreign exchange from the CBN, tend to create false impressions on profitability but they are not sustainable.

**d. Opaque Operations:** The Nigerian carriers have a practice of not declaring profits or losses all year round. It is, however, generally believed that they are not liquid but rather in debt. Apart from ADC and Medview Airlines that got listed on the Nigerian Stock Exchange (NSE), the other airlines are not. It is shady and suspicious too, that in the first year of MedView's Annual General Meeting, huge profit was declared, only for the airline to halt operations thereafter. Could it be that the company winded up flight operations in order to declare profits or was it another case of funds diversion? A suspicion on "cutting corners." It is important for all those at the helm of affairs in the aviation industry and the Nigerian government as well, to re-evaluate policies guiding the operations of the sector so that strategies on how to move the country's aviation industry forward can be brought to bear, and position the airlines adequately for global competitiveness.

**e. Productivity is Affected:** Unethical behavior affects theproductivity of employees. In an ethical corporate culture, employees are more likely to report incidents of wrong-doing to their managers. When an organization recognizes that there is malfeasance (wrong doing) that can lead to the drain of resources, such can be nipped in the bud. For example, employees may lie about assets, funds in expense/suspense accounts and falsify the number of hours they worked thus, creating further drain on workplace productivity and revenue base. The point is that, an unethical business culture where duplicity and or secrecy are common place breeds waste, and productivity is affected.

Generally, in an economy characterized by high unemployment rate, inflation, sharp practices, and lack of dignity and merit, most managers can hardly insist on business ethics as required by the laws of the land. These are the challenges many employees and business owners face. They have to make tough decisions that have farreaching results. Thus, fairness and honesty are big issues. Again, because of the fluidity of poor ethics, some individuals do make wrong business decisions which they consider to be right.

**f. Short Life-Span:** Experts believe that most indigenous airlines experience short life-span because owners or operators of such airlines do not understand the peculiarity of the Nigerian business environment. The trend, after the deregulation of the local air travel industry in the 1980s, provided for free entry and free exit for all. But many times, the euphoria and ego-tripping only lasted for few years. The harsh realities begin to show up with the challenges of routine overseas maintenance, corresponding bills, taxations, and debt repayments. A careful assessment reveals that cost is permanently higher than income. Also, other challenges such as tax overburden and infrastructural deficits, clearly show that government is at variance with the survival of airline players. The continuous erosion of revenue and profits remain steady till such a time that airlines are forced to fold up.

**g. Lack of Professional Managers and Compliance to Rules:** In most airlines in the Nigerian aviation industry, some professionals are lacking behind in competence and technological skills required in today's vibrant and fast changing technological space. For example, a pilot who is expected to rest after two trips done locally back-to-back is forced to keep up with more flights without rest because the airline is not willing to employ more qualified hands but seeks to maximize the available competent pilot at the detriment of the pilot's health. This is a poor reflection of bad crew rostering when there are software today that can prepare the roster seamlessly in compliance with the regulations. Also, such staff could be coerced by management or enticed with increased allowances. They will subsequently not log-in their flights in a bid to follow management's desire to keep flying and cutting corners. Indeed, the airline operations in Nigeria should not be a "tea party" for a few sole-ownership firms, but a deliberate synergy of small firms, coming together, by pooling their resources. This can do the magic of revamping the aviation industry with more profit-oriented airline players.

# CHAPTER TWELVE

# SAFETY AND GROUND MAINTENANCE:
## Flying Coffins

B ack in 1971, I was a very vibrant young chap with the will to explore. Growing up in a suburb in Lagos, it was always fun seeing airplanes fly over my high school.

Holidays were usually the time for all forms of creative display of art works and scientific experiments by young people who, just like me, had great aspirations and dreams. Some of us designed and created colourful flying kites made of nylons, ropes, and sticks, and controlled by yarns for sewing. We flew those kites with friends and absolutely enjoyed playing with them.

The brilliance with which these kites were flown high up in the sky made me imagine how awesome it will be someday to be aboard an aircraft gliding at high speed through the clouds. I became more enthusiastic about flying, having learnt that air transport is the fastest and safest means of transport. I got to know that some commercial jets can reach speeds of up to 954 kilometers per hour (593 mph), and a considerably higher ground speed if there is a jet stream tailwind; while piston-powered general aviation aircrafts may reach up to 555 kilometers per hour (345 mph) or more.

According to Sir Isaac Newton, "What goes up must come down." This is true to a very large extent, but what scared the hell out of me as a child was the way some kites sometimes fell uncontrollably from the skies. And for this singular reason, sometimes I would reconsider my quest to someday soar aboard any flying metal. I feared that it could drop from the sky like a kite gone out of control, having lost contact with the yarn used to navigate it from the ground. But to put my fears to rest, the National Center for Health Statistics estimates the average person's odds of dying in a plane crash at 1 in 20,000 as compared to dying in a car accident (1 in 100).

Noteworthy is the fact that safety in the global aviation industry is paramount. Commercial flight operations are highly regulated in most countries and airplanes must pass extensive tests before being approved for flight. However, the incessant reports of crashes leading to loss of lives continually tainted the credibility of travelling by air and narrowed my chances of attempting to board an airplane.

Just like road accidents, air accidents were increasingly becoming a common phenomenon in Nigeria. As a result, whenever a plane crashes, the national flag would be lowered in honor of the dead. In most instances, apart from this symbolic action, nothing tangible would be done by our leaders to ameliorate the conditions that led to the plane crashes. I would be expecting the government to take the bull by the horn and make sweeping problem-solving changes, but mine was (and is) a nation suffering greatly from lack of infrastructural investment as a result of massive corruption. At the earlier stage, in the 1960s, Nigeria used to have a well- managed aviation industry in the country with a national carrier, the Nigeria Airways.

At the time, corruption was not pervasive and money allocated for airplane maintenance was used accordingly. Then, Nigerians working in the aviation industry were dedicated and conducted themselves in a professional manner. Consequently, the Nigeria Airways had both domestic and international flights that conveyed Nigerians within and outside the country extensively in the glorious days of the industry.

Of course, during those days, privately owned indigenous commercial airline businesses were non-existent since the Nigeria Airways, a government-owned airline was probably the only domestic passenger carrier service. Most of the privately operated airplane and helicopter services were foreign-owned. These private air services provided services to companies that needed air transportation.

Unfortunately, the saying, "nothing lasts forever" became the reality of the Nigerian aviation industry. From the mid-80s, as corruption became the major national occupational pastime, the ability of Nigeria Airways to operate professionally and effectively became questionable. Corruption ate into the very fabric of our society like ringworm on a mission to kill its host. Money allocated for operations and maintenance of Nigeria Airways was diverted into private pockets of leading government officials as concerns about the long-term devastating effects of cutting corners were shrugged off. By the early 90s, Nigeria Airways could not even pay for its airport rental spaces in various major cities of the world, and eventually had to cancel its services.

Sadly, one could recall in 1994 that some Nigerians living in the USA, tired of flying in other national airlines, decided to fly the Nigerian Airways for a planned visit to their country. They waited endlessly at the John F. Kennedy Airport but the plane never arrived from Lagos and the airline's officials kept giving different explanations as to why the scheduled flight to Lagos could not take place. Frustrated, those passengers who had enough money took other airlines to Nigeria while those without enough money got temporarily stranded at the airport before finding their way to Nigeria. It was a very sad and disappointing experience for these proud Nigerians as they watched citizens of other countries fly in their national airlines and Nigerians could not enjoy such an opportunity.

Many Nigerians at the airport wondered why a country like Nigeria could not effectively manage an airline when even very small Caribbean Island nations could do so successfully.

When I read about the alarming occurrences of death that were associated with airline travels over the years, I became the more traumatized. Most recorded cases of airplane accidents were due to human error (50%-60%); air cargo traffic especially in military aviation constituted 65%-75%; accidents involving commercial passenger flights constituted about 3.1%; those involving noncommercial transport constituted 86%; while 2.4-14.2% cases of airline accidents remained unclear. Mechanical failure, airframe deficiencies, meteorological conditions, and inefficient technical servicing were listed as other causes of fatalities in the aviation industry. *Take- off* and *landing* are the phases of flights where air accidents occur the most (most accidents occur in the immediate vicinity of airports). While 50% of air accidents with fatal injuries occur during landing, 20% - 25% occur during take- offs.[21] "No one is above mistakes," is a popular saying that makes it convincingly glaring that human error eclipses all other factors associated with airline fatalities. Since these factors are usually characterized by operating errors such as negligence, complicated control switches or lack of professionalism in handling threatening situations.[22]

Remarkably, as a way of suppressing technical issues, the recent advancements in technology have fitted modern planes with highly effective safety features that prevent catastrophic failures mid-flight. In spite of the several preventive measures proffered, the human element poses difficulty in combating airline maladjustment because humans are highly complex and are bound to make mistakes due to the error of commission or omission, or outright negligence. Although major pilot error happens rarely, the results can be truly devastating and grievous.[23]

As Nigeria Airways was being sacrificed on the altar of corruption, privately owned indigenous commercial airlines began to emerge in Nigeria. Thus, it could be inferred that the private airline business in Nigeria is a direct and indirect beneficiary of the collapse of the publicly owned Nigeria Airways. This means that corruption probably had a major role in providing the ability of some Nigerians to own private airlines in the country.

Most high-level public officials in Nigeria have traveled abroad, yet they approve the construction of airports that do not meet contemporary international airport design standards. A very careful examination of the Abuja, Port Harcourt, Enugu, etc. airports shows that they are substandard. For example, apart from the Murtala Mohammed Airport, Nigerian airports have toilets that would make you think you are in an airstrip in the middle of a forest. The toilets in the domestic airports are comparable to an abandoned biochemical laboratory with a sickening foul odor and are indeed filthy. The stomach-churning odor would make time in the place quite unbearable.

In addition, it is necessary sometimes for passengers to carry along toilet papers otherwise, they could easily end up in a toilet without toilet paper to use. These toilets stink like skunks and the only explanation for the official acceptance of these substandard airports is that the public officials – saddled with the responsibility of ensuring standards – received kickbacks from the contractors to cut corners and execute shabby jobs.

Another worrisome thing is the lax security systems. Most of the airports have no secured perimeter fencing and this means that people and animals can walk directly into the path of an incoming plane thereby causing fatality. It is not surprising that at a time, cows almost collided with planes in Lagos, Port Harcourt, Akure, etc. It is quite unfortunate that large sums have been spent to put up these airports that are merely elongated airstrips. These big budget projects end up looking like something built by unskilled laborers. Recently, the Enugu State government directed officials of Enugu East Local Government Council to immediately close down Orie Emene Market and find a suitable site for the relocation of the market. This is after FAAN had threatened to either close down the Akanu Ibiam International Airport, Enugu, or withdraw its international status.

The minister of state, aviation, Mr. Hadi Sirika, had complained about the presence of the market close to the airport which he said attracted birds. He was quoted as saying that the presence of birds caused constant bird strikes, and that the placement of the state radio mast directly facing the runway, posed security and safety challenges to the airport.[24]

## 1. ADDRESSING THE PRIMARY CAUSES OF AVIATION ACCIDENTS

Interestingly, air travel has an infinitesimal 0.07 deaths per one billion passenger miles.[25] This may be linked – in part – to advancement in technology, judging by the many safety features incorporated into the design and engineering of the latest Airbus and Boeing planes. Safer air travels have also been a result of the other mechanisms that have been put in place such as planning, control and effective monitoring of all airlines' activities. However, the rising doubt for aviation safety due to fatal air crashes and reported cases of deaths coupled with factors like unfavorable weather conditions, enemy invasion, hijacking, military attacks across borders and technical malfunctioning at some point, drained my interest and enthusiasm for the adventure of flying aboard airplanes in the skies.

I duly observed that the causes of air accidents are not fortuitous events, but can be classified in one or several of the following five groups of causes:

1. Human (pilot, other flight personnel, flight safety personnel)
2. Mechanical (aircraft, facilities on the ground)
3. Environment (atmosphere)
4. Mission (flight contract, objective, time, freight, fuel)
5. Management (flight organization, maintenance).[26]

Truly, *what goes up surely comes down,* but it is not as simple as the words imply in the aviation industry when unplanned *coming down* would mean death of loved ones, loss of valuable properties and decline/complete collapse of business fortunes. And the frequency with which these planes drop from the skies (in the Nigerian airspace) like lifeless birds is the reason some people called them "flying coffins." at one time in history of Nigeria.

It has over the years raised questions on the functionality of planes and credibility of airlines, especially when the reasons for such crashes are reported. Few years back, on June 3, 2012 precisely, a DANA aircraft crashed into buildings in Lagos while attempting an emergency landing, killing all 153 people on board and 6 on the ground within few minutes to landing.[27]

What demoralizes me the most about this quantum loss of lives and properties is the fact that political feuds between countries constantly negate the safety of air travels as this was evident in the accident of February 18, 2018, with a record of 65 passengers and crew members dead in Iran. The US sanctions prevented Iranian air carriers from upgrading their fleets of passenger planes that should have been changed ten years back. This forced Iranian Air companies to rely on an aging airline fleet, on spare parts purchased from the black market, and on second- rated Russian planes. Much of the Iranian airplanes predated the 1979 revolution with a life expectancy of 30 years.

Regrettably, bad weather and engine problems due to technical failure were, at some point, given as the possible reasons for the accident. According to the BBC, Iran had experienced about 200 accidents involving planes and suffered almost 2,000 lives lost, in more than two decades.[28]

During the 2015 electioneering period in Nigeria, at the South- South presidential rally of his party at the Liberation Stadium, Port Harcourt, the All Progressive Congress, APC, presidential candidate, General Muhammadu Buhari (Rtd), opined that "If we don't kill corruption, this corruption will kill us."

The fact that the APC government has done little or next to nothing to kill corruption in Nigeria after almost completing two tenures after Buhari's assertion, does not negate the truth of his statement. Therefore, suffice it to say that, the rot in the aviation industry is as a result of heightened corruption, gross ineptitude, mismanagement, carelessness and unprofessionalism of some aviation personnel.

Over the years, we have configured the polity to absorb our self-inflicted woes while confidence in the aviation industry has eroded alarmingly. The disarrayed state of aviation industries, especially in the developing countries, raises concern continually.

For instance, the reported cases of inferno in aircraft emergency exit doors, smoke engulfing planes on motion, control or panel switches malfunction, and cattle occupying runaways, coupled with the incessant hike in airline fares, are indications of a wrong way of doing things.

On April 18, 2017, about 20 minutes after take-off, panic struck passengers as smoke engulfed Aero Contractors flight NG 316 from Port Harcourt to Lagos and thereafter there was another collision between Air Peace and Dana Air flights from Lagos to Port Harcourt on April 21, 2017. How could such things be happening in our industry with so much regulatory instruments?

## 2. SYSTEM AND GROUND MAINTENANCE

The need for aircraft maintenance cannot be over emphasized because of the comfort and safety of both the crew members and passengers on each flight. Aircraft maintenance operations are broadly distributed within and across nations and are performed by both military and civilian mechanics.

Aircraft mechanics work, take place at the airports, maintenance bases, private fields, military installations and aboard aircraft carriers. In general, aircraft maintenance can be divided into **line** and **base maintenance**.

*Base maintenance* includes activities which require the aircraft to be taken out of service for long periods and requires special equipment only available in a hangar. *Line maintenance* activities are mostly carried out during normal turn-around (i.e. the interval between landing and take-off) periods when the aircraft is on the ground. During line maintenance, the aircraft is not always taken out of service and the maintenance activities can be done at the gate or stand itself (or in a hangar if time permits).

According to Delta TechOps Program Manager, Beadle, "Years ago no one really paid much attention to the cost of aircraft maintenance. It was all part of doing business."

But recently, outsourcing aircraft maintenance has become an accepted way for companies to reduce costs and focus on more important issues - core competencies. It is a business-critical activity with regards to strategic importance and finances. What makes outsourcing of aircraft maintenance unique is that lives are potentially at risk if maintenance is not done properly as aircraft maintenance is now viewed as a non-core business.

Furthermore, some air carriers have decided to outsource maintenance rather than establish maintenance operations from scratch and this maintenance outsourcing trend is well established.[29]

In the view of Jetstar Asia's Head of Engineering, Neo, he indicated that he wanted "a Maintenance Repair and Overhaul (MRO) provider with the capability to provide a full suite of engineering services, including a proven and strong ability to provide Aircraft on Ground (AOG) recovery from technical breakdowns."[30]

What actually informed this piece were the pictures of national carriers of some smaller African countries like Air Zimbabwe, Kenyan Airways, Ethiopian Airlines and Ghana Airways that are vibrant in the skies, while all that remains of the once mighty Nigeria Airways are relics – if at all you will see any of them.

Unlike base maintenance which is always scheduled for longer ground times due to periodic check, general overhauling, and refurbishing of the aircraft, line maintenance cannot always be scheduled, since it can imply dealing with unplanned issues arising during normal flight operations.

In line with the foregoing statement, my pastor would say, "success is when opportunity meets preparation" therefore, being wellprepared for unplanned maintenance is fundamental to getting an aircraft back into service quickly after experiencing a technical issue in order to avoid unnecessary delays and cancellations of scheduled flights. Basically, all the information that is necessary to perform a maintenance task is to be found in the maintenance manual or information system.[31]

Additionally, the inspection of aircraft has become much more important because safety is vitally dependent on the detection of very small cracks associated with the onset of multiple site damages. With the improved component designs, focused inspection and maintenance are essential in ensuring the safety of aircraft.

Conversely, in Nigeria, the culture and philosophy underlying business investment is geared towards generating immediate profit. Nigerians tend to invest in businesses that will earn immediate profit. As a result, they rarely plan for long-term consequences. Hence, private airline owners operate their businesses without minding cutting corners in order to generate immediate profits. Sometimes, contractors too cut corners and execute inferior jobs that fall apart within a few years.

The country has major cities across all geopolitical zones, with ever increasing populations yet, the airports in the country do not reflect the rate of population expansion, industrialization, urbanization, and economic growth. Just like in commercial road transportation where old vehicles are recycled to cut down on costs, airline owners seem to negatively cut down costs by buying recycled, retired, and junky planes that have been discarded by their previous owners. These planes are then repaired and repainted to make them look new and they are taken to Nigeria to unwittingly serve and are ridiculously described as commercial flying coffins.

Unfortunately, we – as a nation – have a poor maintenance culture as some corrupt unscrupulous individuals, like ravenous sharks, acting in line with this mediocre social conditioning, would see nothing bad in opening their mouths to swallow dedicated funds, cut corners, and damn the consequences.

When that happens, the Economic and Financial Crimes Commission (EFCC) would come in – making a show of prosecution – but these shows are usually dead ends; the money is already gone and this has always been the culture that has eaten deep into the fabrics of our society. The same corruption that killed Nigeria Airways also killed the Nigerian National Shipping Line (NNSL) and Nigeria Railways. Furthermore, our nation is also known for embarking on white elephant projects that are only meant to be successful on paper. These projects typically serve as conduit pipes for political jobbers, a way of siphoning funds from the public treasury and indirectly impoverishing the people.

According to Mohammed Jibrin, CEO of PEN Aviation Services, a private aviation consultancy firm in Abuja, the Nigerian Civil Aviation Authority is not living up to its expectations. A lot of things are going wrong within the agency, there are lots of sharp practices going on behind the public façade of success. The mandatory training for personnel is a far cry from global best practices and there are cover-ups for their nefarious acts. "The signing out of an aircraft was done very irregularly and the inspections before the importation of aircraft are done very shabbily," Jibrin added. According to him, pervasive corruption has made it possible for airline operators to circumvent measures put in place in line with global best practices.[32]

Additionally, private commercial planes in Nigeria are also part of this sad reality of not being properly maintained before they are deployed into the airspace. The owners, lured by the prospects of quick profits, would not want their planes to remain inactive or idle for too long, so they do unethical things. Consequently, the tired and old planes are not subjected to the kind of repairs that could ensure that they remain airworthy for a long time. It is, therefore, not surprising that these overused planes, like very sick and tired birds, fall off the sky and doom the lives of their occupants. The planes used for domestic flights are too old and not well-maintained. Therefore, flying in them could be akin to a suicide mission or the game of Russian roulette.

Against the backdrop of the massive corruption and ineptitude that has crippled Nigerian institutions for years, the decision by the federal government to suspend the much-advertised new national airline *Nigeria Air*, is a positive step in the right direction.

The dead Nigeria Airways was a metaphor of everything that was wrong with Nigeria. It represented how not to run corporate Nigeria. It is therefore amazing how President Muhammadu Buhari, who had vowed to wipe out corruption, was scheming to revive a corruption cesspit in the name of national pride. It would be paradoxical, indeed ironic and contradictory, for the Buhari administration that was elected on the mantra of anti-corruption to begin to exhume rotten institutions that personified corruption, with the aim of reviving them.

In 2012, virtually all the private airlines operating in Nigeria were at the verge of collapsing due to corruption until the Asset Management Corporation of Nigeria (AMCON) came to their rescue with a N132 billion lifeline. Since then, these airlines have been struggling to remain in business. And in 2014, the debt portfolio of five of the private airlines with AMCON stood at over N190 billion. This is apart from indebtedness to the Federal Airports Authority of Nigeria (FAAN), the Nigerian Airspace Management Agencies (NAMA), other suppliers & institutions.[33]

Unlike commercial road transportation business which is not effectively regulated, aviation is highly regulated but regulation is weakened through corruption. The owners of these private airlines are very powerful individuals in Nigeria and have the political and financial clout to shut down regulatory effort.

Corruption has made it difficult or virtually impossible to regulate the private airline industry effectively. Nigerians should not be surprised that commercial airplanes are crashing more often in the country because the chicken has come to roost after decades of neglect engendered by massive corruption. Just as thousands die or are maimed on the un-kept roads, Nigeria's commercial aviation is increasingly becoming a deathtrap for those traveling by air due to lack of airport development, airplane maintenance, ineffective regulations, and haphazard management of the business.[34]

Accidents do occur, but most airplane mishaps could have been averted. Aviation accidents are caused by a number of factors, ranging from machine deficiencies to incorrect decisions made by humans and environmental issues. Machines do fail from time to time, and human beings who operate the machines are prone to errors, and then the influence of the environmental conditions as well. Some of these factors we can control but some are out of our control. It is sad and gloomy when an accident occurs and lives are lost, yet the fact is that some accidents are avoidable and they wouldn't have happened if all the safety measures had been promptly observed and applied.

Around the world, most governments have adopted a hands-off approach to the running of national airlines or at best have minority shares in private-public arrangements. However, it is baffling how Nigeria that is still battling with mundane issues wants to solely run a national carrier. The Nigerian administrative environment, at the moment, is not aviation friendly. The many administrative and operational bottlenecks function like parasites on businesses, hence, the fumbling of several airlines operating in the country.

Our airports, whether international or domestic, are an eyesore. The Lagos International Airport Road alone could scare visitors and investors because of the decadence the supposedly international gateway advertises. The road networks in the country are dark alleys until they are rehabilitated. The international airline operators had on many occasions bemoaned the decay that characterized Nigerian airports - offices, parking lots, arrival and departure halls, conveniences, insecurity, etc.

Inarguably, the three major international airports in Lagos, Abuja and Port Harcourt, have consistently been rated among the worst in the world and the corruption that led to aviation bankruptcy is still rife. The future of aviation and airlines in Nigeria, according to experts, are among the most vulnerable in the world and incites global and local shocks. Irrefutably, if the Nigerian government is interested in aviation, it should focus on providing an enabling environment by way of restructuring and modernizing the facilities at the airports and making them meet international standards and the roads leading to the airports need to be expanded and maintained to cut down traffic jams. Private airlines should be encouraged to operate under laid down regulations for effective service delivery and the facilities in these airports need to be upgraded to international standards. Therefore, Lagos, Port Harcourt, Abuja, Kano, Calabar, Maiduguri, Kaduna or Sokoto, and Enugu should have airports capable of handling international as well as local flights. By the way, tolls to airports should be discontinued for passenger pick up and drop off since cars that parked will eventually make payments for parking.

The regulatory apparatus should investigate the age of the planes used to carry domestic passengers in Nigeria. They should probe the maintenance records of these planes in an effort to determine the level and quality of repairs and services made on the planes and nonairworthy airplanes should not be allowed to fly as commercial vehicles in the country's airspace.

If the aforementioned actions are carried out effectively, airplane crashes would be drastically minimized, even though absolute safety is never guaranteed.

Based on the highlighted issues that have bedeviled the Nigerian aviation industry, Nigeria should try to get into the modern age in air transportation and stop behaving like a colony that needs only airstrips and re-engined old planes to carry its citizens.

More time should be expended on fixing the problems associated with air transportation. If these problems are fixed, then we can convincingly say that our airspace is devoid of flying coffins and the perception of reliability would inspire more people to patronize the aviation industry, thereby strengthening the Nigerian economy.

# CHAPTER THIRTEEN

# INNOVATIVE TECHNOLOGY:
## The Paradox

*#Technology trust is a good thing,*
*but control is a better one" – Srephane Nappo*

W hen you think about innovation, you think about ideas, which are the seeds of innovation, and this century is filled with many examples of ideas that have been birthed and now rule the information technology space. The Business Dictionary defines innovation as "the process of translating an idea or invention into a good or service that creates value or for which customers will pay." Further, before innovation could be said to have taken place, it must be possible to replicate the same idea at an economical cost, towards satisfying a specific need.[35] When the process of translating such an idea or invention into a good or service is done with the aid of technology, it is referred to as a technological innovation, or an innovative technology. The global aviation industry has continued to grow through many challenges that arise from a complex framework of risks, vulnerabilities, threats, and insufficiencies. These challenges have implications for security, safety, sustainability, customer satisfaction, policy/regulatory effectiveness, and travel optimization. In a quest for solutions to these challenges across various fronts in the aviation business, many innovative ideas have been born, powered by modern technological capabilities. The final products of these have been widely and effectively harnessed for a more robust aviation business in several countries.

Some of the applications of innovative technologies in modern aviation include the more common ones that are built into aircrafts, which help to lift it into the air, and sustain it there throughout the duration of the flight. Such include jet propulsion engines, flight and air traffic control systems/computers, etc.; other technologies include augmented and virtual reality technologies that are used in flight simulations to train pilots, as well as help passengers navigate through airports.

Biometric technologies used to uniquely identify individuals associated with flight operations for security applications and artificial intelligence that helps to learn more about customers and their preferences so as to provide a better flying experience, are some of the few worthy of mentioning.

All these applications of innovative technologies in modern aviation have brought great benefits to the global aviation industry, especially as it pertains to efficiency, profit maximization, effective safety and security, and improved client satisfaction. For example, before Lawrence Burst Sperry developed the "Automatic Flight Control System" (AFCS) in 1932, also known as autopilot, fatigue was a great concern for the safety of passengers and flight crew especially on long international flights across countries, continents, and large oceans, since it was impossible for pilots and flight officers to stay awake and remain alert for long hours on such flights, and still maintain the minimum level of efficiency that is required to safely fly an aircraft. Today, the AFCS has become an indispensable composite of avionics (the collection of "electronic systems, equipment and devices [that are] used to control key systems of the plane and its flight)" of modern aircrafts that are operated in global aviation.[36]

# 1. OVERVIEW OF INNOVATIVE TECHNOLOGIES IN GLOBAL AVIATION

The global aviation industry has been enriched by various innovative technologies that have been of immense benefit in boosting the reputation of the industry in the areas of efficient service delivery and customer satisfaction.

Robotic technologies have been deployed in several airports to take charge of baggage checks, loading luggage and cargo into the cargo deck of aircrafts. Closed circuit cameras (CCTV) with built-in facial recognition technology have been used to identify persons, as well as monitor movement and suspicious behaviors and activities exhibited by passengers and staff within airport premises.

Biometric technologies are also being used across many international airports to verify the identity of travelers at ports of entry and exit. X-ray technologies are now being used to efficiently screen baggage for contraband and prohibited items. Body scanners and metal detection doors are now used to inspect body areas of travelers for dangerous metallic objects and wearable explosives, prior to boarding a flight. In addition to this, software technological solutions such as billing settlement systems built with block-chain technology are used to facilitate the provision of payment services and interactions among various aviation stakeholders. Unmanned aerial / autonomous vehicles (UAVs), also known as drones, are also being used at airports to search for lost individuals and missing items, to inspect maintenance activities, as well as provide directions to travelling parties; de-icing fluids applied to aircraft wings, which help the aircraft to cope at high altitudes in the presence of frost build-ups around the wings. Indoor positioning systems (known as beacon technology) have been used to locate objects and people in real-time within airports.

Moreover, cloud computing and big data analytics have helped to bring together airline clients and operators in ways that ensure that both parties co-habit the aviation industry in a mutually beneficial manner. Mobile and other ubiquitous computing technologies have also amplified the convenience of service delivery in the aviation business, especially with regards to flight booking, managing travel itinerary, and selecting from a wide repertoire of other airline services including rental, scheduling pickups, and drop-offs, etc. This empowers both clients and airline service providers alike in ways that were hitherto unprecedented. Sensor systems and tracking technologies have also been applied extensively in monitoring the flight path, and aerodynamic activities of aircrafts during flights. Assistive technologies that help disabled travelers navigate through the airport and board their flights without hitches are being implemented. Natural language processing and translation technologies that help non-indigenous travelers communicate and understand information around airports, and on board aircrafts are now expedient. Prior to the advent of technology, emotional support animals such as "seeing eye dogs "to help the blind navigate were used.

Furthermore, 5G communication technologies have also started rolling out at several airports to facilitate machine-machine, humanhuman, and human-machine communications at high-speeds, and in real-time. These present an overview of the more popular innovative technologies that have continued to revolutionize the modern aviation business. In the next section I will explain in greater detail the specific benefits and advantages that these technologies bring into global aviation and the portended risks for aviation businesses.

## 2. INNOVATIVE TECHNOLOGIES: RISKS AND BENEFITS

Modern innovative technologies present many obvious advantages and benefits for the global aviation industry. Topmost among these have been:

a.  *Scalability*: aviation businesses have been able to leverage innovative technologies to upscale their service delivery, and grow a global customer base in ways that might previously have been thought to be impossible with much ease and efficiency. This has made it possible for smaller airlines to nurture and manage a global reputation by effectively leveling the playing field, so that long-standing and more- experienced 'hippos,' as well as young and emerging 'gazelles' can compete fairly.

b.  *Cost Reduction*: modern aviation businesses have been able to scale at will, and along broad or marginal spectra while still not 'breaking the bank'. This is attributable to the reductions in associated costs and funding they have enjoyed by integrating innovative technologies across various aspects of their operations. For example, through electronic ticketing systems, billing settlement plans and customer data analytics, airlines have been able to render more convenient and tailored services to their clients while cutting costs that might have ordinarily been associated with market surveys, additional ground personnel, and compensation costs for flight delays and cancellations, to mention a few. Huge cost was cut from acquisition, processing and storage of paper works of tickets, airway bills, shippers letter of instructions (SLIs), excess baggage, etc. They are all electronically processed today.

c.  *Environmental Sustainability*: in the modern era of sustainable growth, the integration of innovative technologies into global aviation has continued to contribute in no small measure to environmental sustainability. For example, fully-electric, turboelectric and hybrid-electric jet propulsion systems are now being built into aircrafts to replace the reliance on fossilized fuels and energy options with renewable alternatives. Air and noise pollution is reduced giving birth to environment that is cleaner and neater.

d. *Mobility and Ubiquity of Information*: Innovative technologies have also enabled the mobility and ubiquity of information on-demand. This has greatly benefited the global aviation industry that relies in no small measure on accurate information (such as details on weather, global positioning, natural elements and phenomena, etc.) that must be up-to-date, and available in real-time.

e. *Effectiveness and Efficiency*: Some risks to the aviation business by the susceptibilities and predispositions of the human employee have been greatly mitigated by the integration of innovative technologies. Fraud, crime, fatigue, morbidity, mortality, and other propensities of the human worker can all be effectively contained or minimized by the strategic and systematic incorporation of technological innovations.

Of course, there is always another side to every beautiful story. Therefore, innovative technologies also come with critical risks that could rock aviation businesses and entire industries if not carefully taken into consideration. Some of these risks include the following points.

f. *Unemployment and Reduced Worker Morale*: Since information technology tends to reduce dependence on personnel and human workforce, the legitimate fear of machines replacing people at their jobs could result in low morale among the workforce which could subsequently cause disloyalty, corporate espionage, and susceptibility to insider threats and attacks.

g. ***Cyber Threats and Attacks***: Many innovative technologies rely on cyber-powered infrastructure to function effectively. This invariably increases the vulnerability of aviation businesses to cyber threats and attacks, some of which could be terror-or politically-motivated. Thus, aviation industries that continue to progressively integrate innovative technologies into their operations must also begin to take the duty of cybersecurity rather seriously. These are but a few of the more common benefits and risks that innovation technologies are able to bring into the global aviation business.

Evidently, as can be seen, the benefits far outweigh the risks. When you really look at it, the days with these innovative technologies are not totally problem-free but innovation has proven to be quite beneficial. What should be done is to address the new challenges that arise as a result of new and better ways of doing things. This might lead one to ask why it yet remains the case that several global aviation businesses and industries have failed to tap into the immense benefits, while establishing structures to diminish the risks, especially for a growing aviation industry like Nigeria's. The next section discusses the dimensions of this reality.

## 3. CONTEMPORARY CHALLENGES

Within the context of the Nigerian aviation industry, many challenges and debates have continued to shadow and polarize discussions regarding the incorporation and implementation of innovative technologies across the various micro-units of the industry. Beginning from the airports, to domestic flight operations, and indigenous airline businesses, the necessity of integrating innovative technologies has been one of the chief concerns of stakeholder technical sessions. Some of the limiting factors that usually pop-up during such sessions, regarding why Nigeria might not be ready for the deployment of innovative technologies across her national aviation industry, are here briefly discussed.

a. **Installation and Maintenance Costs:** The immediate and long-term costs that are typically associated with the acquisition, installation, and maintenance of innovative technologies within Nigeria's aviation industry have remained a foremost agenda for discussion whenever the subject of innovative technologies in aviation pops up. While many experts and stakeholders have continued to decry the dilapidated state of airports around the country, the government has not given the issue the needed commitment and urgency. The technological system would need routine maintenance and upgrade to keep them functioning optimally and efficiently. It would also need trained personnel to put them to work and this excludes the huge costs that are typically associated with acquiring and installing these technological systems. Our industry is no doubt affected by our culture of governance which shows little or no concrete plan for years ahead, so I doubt the readiness of the Nigerian aviation industry to integrate these innovative technologies, with the support of the government and regulatory authorities.

b. **Technical Training:** In many instances, the right and effective use of innovative technologies in aviation requires proper training of operators, systems administrators, and managers. Often times these trainings are quite expensive, and might need to be taken again by relevant personnel as soon as upgrades and updates are made to the technological systems. The failure to undertake and complete such trainings, especially for critical applications like flight and air traffic control, could portend imminent danger for the flying public. As a result of this, many governments of developing countries prefer to tread the manual / legacy, or at best, semi-automated paths of operation, and are not eager to acquire and deploy these innovative technological systems due to the associated training costs and requirements, and the dangers that could be created as a result of defaulting in this regard.

c. **Regulatory and Legislative Preparedness:** Many modern applications of innovative technologies in global aviation, must, of necessity, be regulated by policy, and protected by legislation. For example, applications of artificial intelligence (AI), big data analytics, and robotic technologies are required by global best practices to be safeguarded by regulations and legislation. Contemporary issues regarding the ethics of AI, the secure and ethical use of big data and machine learning, the safety of robotic machines at the interface with human agents, and the security of virtual / augmented reality environments, have now topped the agenda in global discourses regarding the development of innovative technologies for application in various areas of the aviation business. Thus, global best practices now recommend a certain level of regulatory and legislative backbone/preparedness for the safe, secure, ethical, efficient, authorized, and effective use of these innovative technologies, particularly within critical areas of aviation. Not many countries (especially of the developing and underdeveloped worlds) have the robust and flexible regulatory and legislative frameworks that are necessary for engaging effectively with these contemporary issues; thus, they refrain from integrating these innovative technologies into their national aviation industries.

e. **Infrastructural Support:** Many modern innovative technologies rely on vast array of infrastructural support systems in order to function effectively and optimally. Some of these include: high-speed internet connectivity, reliable broadband and satellite communication systems, high-end computing capabilities, accurate global positioning systems and technologies, resilient cybersecurity, and reliable digital (mobile and computer) communication networks. Apparently, such modern infrastructural support is often lacking in many countries, or at best exists in a very unreliable or largely dysfunctional form. Unfortunately, Nigeria happens to be one of such countries and this presents one of the most formidable challenges to effectively deploying innovative technologies within the country's aviation industry.

## 4. INNOVATIVE TECHNOLOGIES AND NIGERIA'S AVIATION INDUSTRY: THE REALITIES

According to the Nigerian Civil Aviation Authority (NCAA), 14.14 million passengers embarked on 222,413 completed flights in 2017. Yet in the face of these statistics, airline operators have continued to decry the poor environment of aviation in Nigeria, and the seeming unwillingness of the government to step in, and ameliorate the current realities. It then becomes arguable that the flying statistics that have been presented by the NCAA in recent years do not adequately reflect the true flying potential of the country's aviation industry, but only show how badly the industry continues to under-serve the flying public. Perhaps, these statistics are only reflections of the resilience of airline and travel businesses to keep the industry afloat, even without the degree of support that is otherwise expected of the government.

Speaking to the press regarding some of the major challenges faced by private airline businesses and operators in Nigeria, the chairman of a leading private airline in the country highlighted high costs of operations amongst the challenges faced by private airlines in the country's aviation industry.[37] On September 7, 2015, the Nigerian

Aviation Handling Company (NAHCO) announced its intention to acquire ground support equipment (GSE) worth 1.5 billion naira to help enhance operations and service delivery across airports in Nigeria.[38] These GSE were reported to include "aircraft passenger steps, self- propelled pallet transporter, belt loaders, wide aircraft cargo loaders, aircraft tow loaders and towable toilet service units.

Others include towable fuel bowsers, pallet dollies, container dollies, baggage trailers, belt loaders and ACUs." Adding that over N11.3bn ($70m) had been expended in the previous 24 months for the acquisition of modern equipment to enhance operations across airports within the country. *Ibid*

However, there is more to the operations and services provided by world-class airports than can be adequately covered by ground support equipment. Innovative technologies, airport infrastructure, service delivery and security, are other crucial areas where the Federal Airports Authority of Nigeria (FAAN) seems to be failing in delivering on their mandates.[39] In addition, despite such huge capital expenditure that has been committed towards enhancing airports in Nigeria, a popular airport survey ranked two of the country's international airports – the Port Harcourt International Airport, and the Lagos Murtala Muhammed International Airport – amongst the top 5 worst airports in Africa in 2017.[40] The local reports and statistics that are published annually by the Federal Airports Authority of Nigeria (FAAN) continue to suggest that all is fun and well at the various airports distributed across the country. In fact, just reading these local reports and statistics, one might be tempted to believe that nothing could be any better than 'good news' being reported about local and international airports in Nigeria, until they are benchmarked against expert and customer ratings, and the global best practices on the -list of airports around the world.

There is need to have an action plan that will assist the industry to attain its expected height. To this end, I have made certain observations. Looking at the facts on ground, it quickly becomes evident that the government is expending her capital resources on the wrong things, and that the government needs to focus on her goals of capital expenditure towards meeting the demands of the modern age.

Unfortunately, this is a reality that continues to be strategically obscured by the reports and statistics that are published periodically by aviation authorities in the country which tend to suggest that it's almost "eureka!" for the country's aviation industry. Therefore, in trying to understand the actual status of the airports in the country, especially with regards to infrastructural efficiency, and service delivery, stakeholders and the government must now consciously shift attention away from these reports and statistics whose sources and data remain questionable. Instead, the opinions and reviews of airport users, personnel and passengers that frequently operate within, and travel through these airports, should be given the needed attention.

Among other benefits, these reviews and surveys would provide comparative perspectives into the country's airports, in relation to other airports across the world. They would help to highlight the major areas of deficiency, and provide recommendations into better ways of enhancing operations and service delivery in line with innovative technologies. An objective consideration of the content of these reviews and survey by relevant local authorities with progressive visions would be able to quickly spot the areas where more capital expenditure efforts are needed, either for the purpose of infrastructural development, technological upgrades, equipment acquisition, systems development, or personnel training.

There is no doubt about the fact that innovative technologies continue to present great benefits and vastly untapped potentials for the global aviation industry, and more so for developing aviation markets like Nigeria; particularly with respect to the areas of long run cost reductions, profit maximization, process optimization, and customer convenience. However, innovators must be wary of unnecessary complexities of technological inventions that would have critical applications on aviation. This is because, as in the words of U.S. President Donald Trump following the Ethiopian Airlines crash of March 2019, pilots should be able to quickly and easily take control of an aircraft in critical situation, and unnecessary complexities in innovation technological systems built into aircrafts could portend serious dangers that might result in fatalities. Not paying due attention to these observations is tantamount to cutting corners.

# CHAPTER FOURTEEN

# SAFETY MANAGEMENT:
## The Nigerian Aviation Story

The aviation system is served by a combination of private service providers and state organizations. This system is required to investigate human roles in ensuring safety and an understanding of how human performance may be affected by its multiple and interrelated components. Safety normally is the quest of every human. Everyone wants to have a feeling of being safe with little or no risk or threat whatsoever. Therefore, safety management in aviation industry are processes put in place which make it possible for risks to be identified, curtailed to the least minimum, and that such processes meet world global acceptable standards. Safest Management System (SMS) as contained in document 9859 is organized into four components which are:

- Safety Policy
- Safety Risk Management
- Safety Assurance
- Safety Promotion

## 1. SAFETY POLICY

Safety policies are put in place to serve as safety regulatory checks. Without a king, a governor or other recognized constituted authorities to enforce laws, citizens of a community will behave as they please, and lawlessness will result to many dangers and acrimony in the society. Safety policies are therefore instituted for management, controls and individual responsibilities. It is expected that at all levels, personnel are to be active players in the implementation of the safety management system. Imagine if a pilot becomes defiant and acts contrary to any of the safety rules, the consequences of such defiance could be very disastrous. It is expedient that airlines and airports organize refresher-training courses periodically to ensure that their staff are always conscious and conversant with policy direction of the organization and what is expected of them at all times. To do the contrary will be cutting corners. Imagine a statement such as "I did not fully understand the guidelines given" coming from a flight pilot. Wouldn't it sound so awkward? Safety policy is the architecture of Safety Management Systems (SMS).

Aviation Safety Management Systems (SMS) are endorsed by the organization's accountable officer or Chief Executive Officer which confirms management's commitment and affords employee protection from self-reporting errors and mistakes. Safety Management System focuses on the following for employees:

- Roles
- Obligations, and
- Guidance in all safety-related circumstances.

It is expedient that aviation safety policy address the following issues adequately:

- Top management's commitment to safety.
- Safety goals and objectives and how they are measured/ monitored.
- Accountable executive's commitment to provide necessary resources for the SMS.

- Expectations of employees and management relating to SMS participation.
- Responsibilities of various roles in the SMS architecture.
- Organization's various approaches to managing safety.
- The hazard reporting policy.
- Employee behavior not protected by the SMS.

It needs to cover everything (within reason) without looking like a complex civil court case analysis. It shouldn't be a tough thing to do, but a relatively short, easy-to-read document.

This is why a typical safety policy:

- Hardly ever adequately touches on all the areas it should
- Could be hard to navigate
- Could be so general as to be meaningless or
- May add no value to the intended audience (the employees).

Before doing anything about drafting safety policy, we must make sure we are clear on the 'Who? What? and Why?' of aviation safety policy. There is considerable guidance on writing safety policy statements.

Unfortunately, safety policy is one of the first tasks that safety managers usually write on behalf of the accountable executive. There is little thought regarding the effect of the safety policy on the organization's *safety culture*. By definition, aviation safety culture is described as reflecting the real commitment to safety, or how people will act when no one is watching. With this understanding, the aviation SMS provides the means to achieve safety, and the *safety culture* is the commitment to achieve safety.

## 2. SAFETY RISK MANAGEMENT

International Civil Aviation Organization (ICAO) safety management approach involves hazard identification, risk assessment and risk mitigation processes and analysis of the processes to such an acceptable or tolerable level that could threaten the viability of an organization.

a.  **Hazard Identification:** This involves deciphering unwanted or adverse events which can result into hazard and the analysis of mechanisms by which these events may happen and cause harm. Reactive and proactive methods should be employed for hazard identification.
b.  **Risk Assessments:** Identified hazards are assessed in terms of how critical their harmful effects are and how they are ranked in order of their risk-bearing potential. They are assessed often by experienced personnel or by utilizing more formal techniques and through analytic methods. The severity and consequences and the likelihood (frequency) of hazardous occurrence are determined. If the risk is considered acceptable, operation continues without any intervention. If it is not, the risk mitigation process is deployed.
c.  **Risk Mitigation:** If the risk is considered to be unacceptable, then control measures are taken to fortify and increase the level of defenses against that risk or to avoid or remove the risk, within economic reach. Tolerating unacceptable non-economic risk level will be cutting corners.

## 3. Safety Assurance

Nigeria (as a growing nation) has come a long way in transportation, evolving from the humble beginning and simplicity of travelling by foot to the sophistication of travelling by air, which is considered to be the fastest and to a great extent the safest means of transportation considering that air accidents are measured per million departures.

According to international air transport association (IATA), 2015 accident rate of 1.79 dropped a to 1.61 in 2016. Frankly, Aviation is considered to be a very safe industry, but how safe is the word "safe" in reality?

As I have noted earlier in the introductory section of this book, the history of aviation in Nigeria dates back to 1925 when the British Royal Air Force landed in Kano for a British intervention in the chaos that happened in Kano and ever since, air travel has become a *cannot-do-without* and a desire of all. However, commercial aviation services between Nigeria and UK took off really in 1935 with flight operated by Imperial Airlines of the UK to serve the British West Africa Colonies. In 1940, the Second World War started precipitating the completion of aerodromes and airports that had been planned for Nigeria and ever since, there has been tremendous growth in the Nigerian aviation system with about 22 airports or more established by the Federal Airport Authority of Nigeria (FAAN) and other locally owned airports across the country. Safety has been considered to be the greatest challenge of the industry.

Indeed, many plane crashes that we've recorded have been majorly traced to human errors and lack of efficient safety management policies – indeed these policy documents are available but not duly followed.

Everyone wants to be safe or to at least have a feeling that risk and hazards can be reduced to the barest minimum. A child looks up to the parents for safety and if the father throws the child up gymnastically, he or she is relaxed and confident that the father would catch him or her on the way down and prevent crashing. I only wish this can be the same for aviation customers and those who operate the industry. We must get to a point when people can experience travelling without having to fidget and without one's heart thumping hard against the chest. The aviation industry may not be absolutely free from hazards because human inventions can never guarantee total safety, but safety can be ensured to a very great extent.

Stating the express priority of IATA, safety is germane and of utmost importance for every flight to take-off and land safely. Any accident recorded throws a big challenge at institutions like the ICAO, IATA, airplane manufacturers, etc. Safety threat caused by either operational failings or human errors frequently result to incidents and or accidents.

a.  **Accident** is defined in International Civil Aviation Organization (ICAO) Annex 13 as an occurrence associated with the operation of an aircraft which takes place from the time any person boards the aircraft with the intention of flight until all such persons have disembarked, and in which:
    - A person is fatally or seriously injured;
    - The aircraft sustains significant damage or structural failure;
    - The aircraft gets missing or becomes completely inaccessible.

b.  **Incident** is defined in Annex 13 as an occurrence, other than an accident, associated with the operation of an aircraft that affects or could affect the safety of operation resulting into NO fatality. Howbeit, most aviation service providers have processes in place to prevent risk to an acceptable level. Emphatically, every operator has a safety management system. But what happens when an operator decides to neglect these processes and rely on impulsive acts or past experience with outdated knowledge and complacency set in? What happens when these processes are seemingly complex beyond comprehension? They could be good on paper but unworkable in reality. Giving these scenarios, accidents or incidents would be inevitable.

To ensure safety, IATA has put up six-point safety strategy focusing on the following key areas:

- **Reduction of operational risks:** It has been found out that operational risks are the greatest concern of any airline. IATA together with various airline experts have identified key safety issues which include cabin safety, runaway safety, fatigue, mid-air collision and other related issues.

- **Enhance quality and compliance:** IATA Operational Safety Audit (IOSA) serves as bedrock approach to enabling aviation safety by using a tool called IMX (Integrated Management Solutions), an efficient and cost-effective solution to manage the collection and processing of information. This is known as safety-data-collection-and- processing system.

- **Advocate for improved aviation infrastructure**

- Support consistent implementation of safety management system

- **Support effective recruitment and training.** This includes: IATA training and licensing, Air Traffic Control (ATC), ground handling agents, classroom and in-company training courses.

- **Identify and address emerging safety issues.**

# 4. SAFETY PROMOTION

Furthermore, ICAO is constantly striving to improve aviation safety performance through the following:

a. The development of global strategies contained in the Global Aviation Safety Plan and the Global Air Navigation Plan.

b. The development and maintenance of Standard and Recommended Practices and Procedures applicable to international civil aviation activities.

c. The monitoring of safety trends and indicators. ICAO audits the implementation of its standard Recommended Practices and Procedures through its Universal Safety Oversight Audit Programme. Likewise, high-tech tools, which can collect and analyze a vast array of safety data, allow the identification of existing and emerging risks.

d. The implementation of targeted safety programmes to address safety and infrastructure deficiencies

e. An effective response to disruption of the aviation system created by natural disasters, conflicts or other causes.

Literally, plane crashes do not only make pointed headlines but they demoralize the affected airline. Therefore, it is clearly evident that safety is really a germane goal of any airline.

Taking a world view, analytical statistics shows that there is a great drop in the number of people killed in plane crashes in 2018 which shows a positive progression in terms of safety and it seems like a silver lining to the aviation industry as a whole.

Nevertheless, it appears that in as much as there is the struggle to eradicate accidents and incidents, the aviation industry might not be totally free of hazards and other safety threats. As noted by Professor James, who developed the Swiss-Model, accidents are caused by incessant breaches of multiple system defenses. These breaches can be as a result of a number of causative factors such as equipment failures or operational errors.

According to industry news published in *ThisDay*, Nigeria has begun the implementation of the State Safety Program (SSP) processes and has achieved good progress with the completion of SSP Gap Analysis and the establishment of implementation plan approved by the director general of NCAA. It was also noted that Nigeria achieved EI level of 67.36 percent during the immediate last ICAO audit in March 2016, which is considered to have exceeded the world average of 63.54 percent.

Notwithstanding this great feat, an operator said the regulatory authority should concentrate now on how to make airline operations in Nigeria profitable in order to ensure continuity and progress in the industry.

# CHAPTER FIFTEEN

# SECURITY MANAGEMENT:
## Gaps and Our Experiences

There is a popular Yoruba saying about gaps and cracks: "Without a crack (or gap) on a wall, a lizard will not be able to find a way into the wall."

My translation of the saying may not be accurate but the message is in no way missing in our context when we look at the way sophisticated criminals have been able to take advantage of the gaps in security management of the Nigerian aviation sector.

On December 24, 2018, Miss Zainab Habibu Aliyu, a Muslim student of Maitama Sule University in Kano State, Nigeria, had set out from Mallam Aminu Kano International Airport (MAKIA) in Kano on a Lesser Hajj – a religious trip to the Muslim Holy Land in Mecca, Saudi Arabia. She had set out on an Ethiopian Airlines flight for the Holy Land in company of her mother, Hajiya Maryam, and sister, Hajara. The flight continued after a brief stop-over at AddisAbaba, Ethiopia on December 25 before continuing to Jeddah, Saudi Arabia, and arriving in the early hours of December 26. Upon arrival at Saudi Arabia, the travelling family was just about to settle in for a deserved rest after a long flight when officials of the Saudi drug agency knocked on their hotel door in Medinah, Saudi Arabia, and arrested Zainab on an allegation of drug trafficking. Zainab, who was shocked and dismayed at the allegation, is said to have continued to uphold her claims to innocence, stating that the substance (believed to be Tramadol) was planted on her.

Now, Saudi Arabia is known to regularly dish out capital punishments for drug-related offences despite international outcry from foreign governments, civil liberty organizations, and humanitarian groups and the death penalty is traditionally carried out by beheading. In a recent statement by the senior special assistant to the president on diaspora, Rt. Hon. Abike Dabiri- Erewa, it was revealed that over fifty Nigerians had already been executed in Saudi Arabia for drug-related offences in the last few months, with at least twenty more currently on death row in the country, and awaiting the execution of their sentences. A petition was filed by Zainab's father, a trained journalist, requesting that the government authorities carry out an investigation into the allegations against Zainab, while also upholding her innocence. The petition was supported by wide campaigns and protests all across Nigeria and abroad by students, and other well-meaning citizens both online and offline.

Thus, the National Drug Law Enforcement Agency (NDLEA) was forced to launch an investigation into the allegation, in response to the petition by Mr. Aliyu and the massive outcry that had trailed the arrest of Zainab while also aware of a recent call by the senior special assistant to the president on diaspora, regarding drug syndicates that had now infiltrated management and staff units of airlines and airports in the country and continue to implicate innocent citizens in various drug-related offences by planting drugs in their luggage.

During the course of investigations, officials of the NDLEA uncovered a drug cartel with seven members who were airport / airline staff at the MAKIA in Kano. In an unfortunate turn of events, a second luggage was planted on Zainab, who set out on the trip with a single luggage that was weighed to have been well below the maximum allowable luggage weight for the flight. It was the extra luggage, which bore a tag with Zainab's name on it that contained the banned substance and the basis for her arrest on December 26 at her hotel room.

Following the outcome of the investigations by the NDLEA, the acting consul-general of the Nigerian Consulate in Jeddah, Saudi Arabia, Garba Satomi Grema, moved quickly to begin diplomatic talks to convince the Saudi authorities of Zainab's innocence, supported by the Ambassador of the Saudi Kingdom to Nigeria, His Excellency Adnan Bin Mahmoud Bostaji, the Nigerian presidency, and other national and international diplomats. On April 30, Zainab Aliyu was released to the Nigerian Consulate in Saudi Arabia, after spending at least four months in detention along with another Nigerian who was released the day after, 74 year old Ibrahim Abubakar, who travelled on the same flight with Zainab on the same day, and had also been implicated in a drug-related offence. The Nigerian authorities had succeeded in convincing the Saudi authorities that both individuals had only been victims of the activities of a wicked drug cartel that specialized in planting drug on unsuspecting travelers to drug zones like Saudi Arabia, Malaysia, Thailand, Indonesia, Singapore, China, United Arab Emirates (UAE) and other countries of the Middle-East, where successful peddling results in high profit despite the risk of execution of innocent individuals who might get caught with the planted contraband.

The duo of Zainab and Ibrahim are the very marginal sample of individuals among a large population of unlucky (though presumably innocent) travelers that ostensibly might have been implicated by the nefarious activities of the busted drug syndicate. While many Nigerians home and abroad have applauded the efforts of the Nigerian government in the swift manner with which they moved to investigate and prove the innocence of these two citizens, effectively saving them from what might have been an unfortunate and untimely death, the emerging evidence from this case has revealed a number of critical areas of vulnerability in the security management processes and procedures of the Nigerian airlines and airports, which could be exploited by malicious individuals to bring the Nigerian civil aviation industry to disrepute. Following the incident, many individuals have now called for urgent reforms, reviews and upgrades to the airport and airline security management processes and procedures by the Federal Ministry of Aviation. Stringent sanctions have been proposed for airlines that are discovered to have been consciously or inadvertently sabotaging the security reputation of the civil aviation business in Nigeria through porous security management practices, especially on Ethiopian Airlines and Egypt Air who have been amongst the major carriers that are patronized by the National Hajj Commission of Nigeria (NAHCON) for transporting Nigerian Muslims on pilgrimages. This is considered necessary in order to redeem the global reputation of Nigerian civil aviation, and forestall a recurrence of such an ignominious incident.

## THE LAYERED APPROACH TO SECURITY MANAGEMENT: AN OVERVIEW

Aviation Security (AVSEC) is guided by International Standard and Recommended Practices (SARPs) contained in Annex 17 to the Convention on International Civil Aviation. The primary objective of AVSEC is to ensure the protection and safety of passengers, crew, ground personnel, the general public, aircraft and facilities of an airport serving civil aviation, against Acts of Unlawful Interference (AUI) perpetrated on the ground or in flight. AUI means an act or attempted act which jeopardises the safety of civil aviation, including, but not limited to:

According to ICAO Annex 17, Acts of Unlawful Interference refers to some acts or attempted acts such as to jeopardize the safety of civil aviation. They include but are not limited to:

- **Forcible intrusion** on board an **aircraft**, at an **airport** or on the premises of an **aeronautical facility.**

- **Unlawful seizure** of aircraft.

- **Hostage-taking on board** aircraft or on **aerodromes**.

- **Destruction** of an aircraft in service.

- **Introduction on board** an aircraft or at an **airport** of a **weapon or hazardous device or material** intended **for criminal purposes.**

- Use of an aircraft in service for the **purpose of causing death, serious bodily injury, or serious damage** to property or the environment.

- **Communication of false information** such as **to jeopardize the safety** of an aircraft in flight or on the ground, of passengers, crew, ground personnel or the general public, at an airport or on the premises of a civil aviation facility.

Perpetrators of Acts of Unlawful Interference are commonly: terrorists (domestic and international); criminals; psychopaths (mentally disturbed) and asylum seekers (refugees); other governments and insiders (company employees – staff).

**Layers of Security**

Layered security is a network security approach that uses several components to protect operations with multiple levels of security measures. The idea behind creating layers of security is to ensure that each component has a backup in case one component fails to detect breach in security.

The most secure airports in the world which include Zurich International Airport, Zurich, Switzerland; Ben Gurion International Airport, Tel Aviv, Israel; Narita International Airport, Tokyo, Japan; King AbdulAziz International Airport, Jeddah, Kingdom of Saudi Arabia; and Changi Airport, Changi, Singapore, implement effective layered security that go a long way in limiting Acts of Unlawful Interferences.

In Dr. H. O. Demuren's 'Perspectives in Multi-Layer Aviation Security System & Passenger Facilitation' presentation paper, he explains:
The three distinct layers of Aviation Security are: Outer Ring, Middle Ring, and Centre Ring. Each layer plays a role in preventing or detecting terrorist attacks at any stage. If one layer fails or is deficient, another will hopefully prevent the Act of Unlawful Interference being successful.

These layers may consist ofsecurity restricted areas;airport identification permits for personnel and vehicles;physical security measures (perimeter fences, gates, locks, patrol etc);detection systems for weapons and explosives. (Demuren 2022)

Figure 1: Aviation Security: Layers of Security

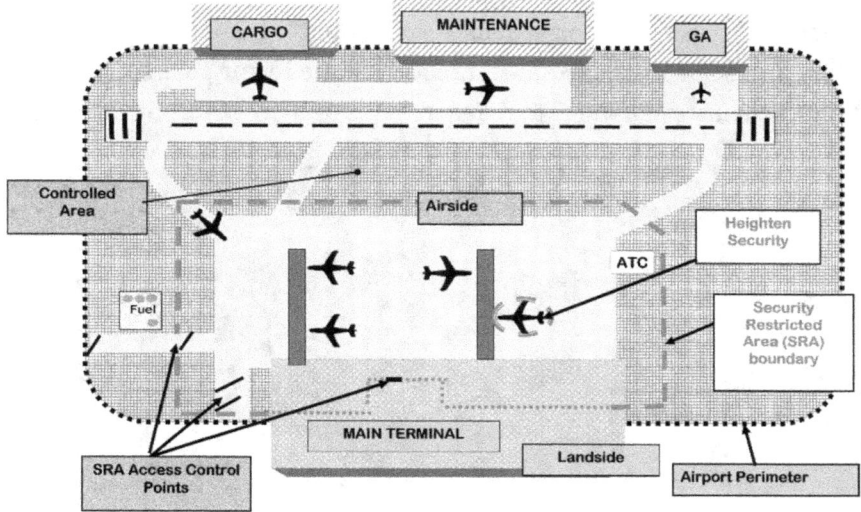

Up until the 1980s, there were no major aviation security challenges in Africa. Then came the 1993 Nigerian Airways hijack (LagosAbuja Flight, diverted to Niamey, Niger Republic). We also had the Umar Farouk Abdul-Mutallab 2010 failed bomb attempt on KLM/NorthWest Airline (Demuren 2022).

Following the destruction of the Twin Towers at the World Trade Centre in the United States on September 11, 2001 with the use of hijacked planes, it became clear, the extent to which terrorists and malicious enemies of state would go to unleash mayhem on innocent and hapless citizens. It became evident that the static approaches to security management and defense that had hitherto been applied were no longer effective in deterring threats and enemies. The modern threat landscape has proven that threat vectors are able to evolve and adapt rapidly and circumvent static security management approaches and defenses. The realization of this fact led the Transportation Security Administration (TSA) to propose and adopt an enhanced, multi-layered approach to security management for the global air transportation industry in order to be able to more effectively deter cross-border threats and attacks that could threaten global peace, safety and security, especially threats that are terror-related. The TSA layered security management approach is shown in the figure below.

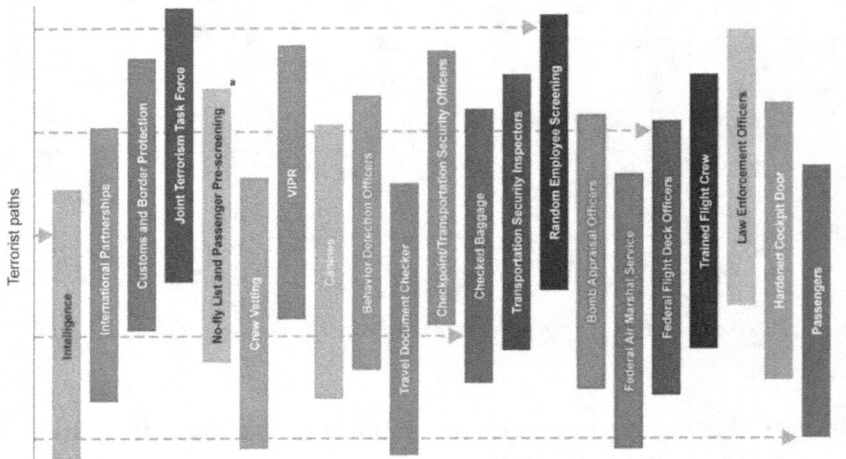

SOURCE: Transportation Security Administration (TSA)

**TSA Layers of Aviation Security**

**William Johnstone**, a transportation security expert and member of the 9/11 Commission staff, in a 2015 article with the US aviation industry in mind:

*The focus on the airport checkpoints has a long history, both before and after 9/11, and is understandable given that this is the most visible, heavily funded, and scrutinized of all transportation security measures. At the same time, security officials state that aviation security is premised on the notion of security layers, of which the checkpoint is only one element, wherein if one layer fails another will support or replace it in thwarting an attack.*

This was against the backdrop of the continued evolution of aviation security structures, systems and regulations in the United States. Today, the Transportation Security Administration (TSA), an agency of the United States Department of Homeland Security (DHS), has 20 integrated components that form its layers of security to keep travelers safe. The layers are both seen and unseen and work like a complex combination safe designed for security.

The TSA Layers of Security progressively specify various officials, responsibilities, tasks, and best practices that can be effectively applied towards security management in aviation. Contextually, these layered procedures can be generally categorized into five modules that comprise critical subsets for robust aviation security management. These five (5) modules are: Intelligence, Baggage Checks, Airport Security and Screening, Flight Deck Security, and Passenger Screening.

## a. Intelligence

*Intelligence* relates to the synergy of the national, regional, and international apparatuses of states and governments to collaboratively identify and correctly profile past, current, imminent, and future threats that could pose dangers to national security, aviation security, and civil safety, especially aboard commercial flights, and share such information for enforcement across borders, jurisdictions, and ports of entry / departure. The efficiency of this module for effective security management is reliant on an elaborate information sharing and feedback mechanism that requires:

i   The formation and strengthening of multi-lateral international partnerships between governments and agencies for effective customs/immigration and border protection, as well as secure trade with international partners.

ii    Joint local, national, or regional task forces to collaborate towards airport security, and ensuring that current structures, practices and operations meet the global standards for security management.

iii   The collation and enforcement of a no-fly list, specifying individuals and groups that have been identified as threats and profiled as (potentially) dangerous entities, and must be kept out of the skies, especially on commercial flights.

iv   Elaborate vetting and proper training procedures for all ground staff and flight crew of airlines, including pilots, engineers, cabin executives.

v   Active teams for "visible intermodal prevention and response" (VIPR), as well as canine squads that are trained to help maximize and complement existing capabilities for detecting harmful, dangerous, and contraband items, and also forestalling imminent security incidents at airports and on- board flights.

vi   Well-trained officers in sociology and psychology, to serve as behaviour detection officers to isolate individuals with

vii  suspicious behavioral dispositions amongst crowds at airports and immigration posts.

viii Personnel that would verify travelers' identification documents and immigration permits, which passengers are required to present at ports of entry/departure of a country; and,

ix   Security officers that would check carry-ons for dangerous / prohibited items before passengers board commercial flights.


## b. Baggage Check

The second module, ***Baggage Check*** relates to all the methods, tools, techniques and technologies that are employed in screening and identifying the baggage/luggage and every other item that is loaded into the cargo compartment of the commercial aircraft. This includes the use of X-ray devices and systems, explosive trace equipment, signal detectors, etc., in carefully scrutinizing baggage/ luggage and cargo for items and materials, pets and animals, reactive/inflammable chemicals, as well as weapons and explosives that could endanger the safety and security of passengers onboard the aircraft. The efficiency of this module for effective security management further requires that transportation security inspectors also carry out extra random checks and confirmations to ensure that the cargo area of the airport is free from malicious individuals and threats that could still compromise baggage / luggage, and cargo that have already passed checking procedures and scrutiny.

## c. Airport Security and Screening

*Airport Security and Screening* relates to security tasks, duties and processes that aim to keep the airport environment safe and secure against possible threats to the travelling public. The efficiency of this module for effective aviation security management is reliant on:

i   Frequent/Routine screening of airport staff and personnel who often gain access to secure areas of the airport, through random daily checks and extensive background assessment of such personnel.

ii  The presence of bomb appraisal officers and diffusion squads who apply advanced security techniques to complement the capabilities of other port-of-entry staff for detecting and disarming explosives. These officers would typically have operational training in the explosives units of the military and law enforcement.

iii Law enforcement officers who are on ground at airports to effect the arrest and detention of passengers found in the possession of prohibited items/substances, as well as help in subduing individuals who display behaviors that could endanger or inconvenience the travelling public.

## d. Flight Deck Security

This module *deals* with all the personnel, structures, and processes that help to ensure the safety and security of travelers while onboard the aircraft. These include:

i   The duties of undercover Federal Air Marshals whose backgrounds have been extensively scrutinized, since they are the one of very few federal officers that are authorized to bear arms beyond the airport waiting area, through the tarmac, and on board an aircraft.

ii  Pilots, and flight officials who are also trained to carry and use firearms during flight operations, as well as being trained in close quarters combat and other forms of self-defense so as to deal effectively with assault and other harmful situations aboard a flight.

iii Hardened cockpit doors, to keep out threats and distractions from the cockpit so that pilots can focus on landing the aircraft during threat / emergency situations, in order to receive support from ground authorities in neutralizing the threat.

## e. Passenger Screening

The fifth and final module, *Passenger Screening,* offers the last line of defense in the aviation security management chain. It involves pre-screening of passengers for small arms, light weapons, harmful glass/metallic objects, and explosives prior to boarding a flight. Sometimes, these screening activities could include pat downs/body searches of passengers by airport and immigration security officers, particularly for individuals who are spotted to feature a suspicious disposition.

Interestingly, this layered approach has been commended for providing a globally- applicable and holistic approach to security management in aviation, which incorporates all stakeholders – airlines, and government authorities, with their personnel and staff, as well as law enforcement, and passengers; in such a manner that creates a complex security system that is more difficult for an attacker or malicious fellow to completely subvert, and outwit.

However, some governments and airline companies have the tendency to relegate certain aspects of the layered-security framework that fall within the jurisdiction of their responsibilities due to high funding / budgetary requirements; particularly with respect to the high-cost equipment and cutting-edge technologies that are required to effectively secure airport premises and ports of entry. The dangers inherent in this relates to the fact that the layered security framework is designed to function as a complex modularized system that feeds back and forth between composite layers. Therefore, any attempt at side-stepping or relegating any of the composite layers could effectively compromise the entire framework and result in devastating security incidents. This will be cutting corners.

## IMPROVED MULTI-LAYER SECURITY MEASURES

To ensure a standard level and safety, some of the enhanced multilayer Aviation Security measures in directives issued by the NCAA to the industry require that:

**a.** No person including crew members should be allowed to board an aircraft without passing through all aviation security screening procedures/formalities and 100% examination is mandatory for all passengers.

b. Secondary screening of passengers and the carry-on baggage should be total and performed for all departing flights at the boarding gates including body search (pat down).

c. It is mandatory to conduct 100% physical inspection of all passengers accessible property at the boarding gate prior to boarding.

d. Liquids, gels, and aerosols should not be allowed on board aircraft without compliance with the requirements of 100ml for liquids and placed in transparent re-sealable plastic bags.

e. 100% screening of checked-in baggage must be performed, and Positive Passenger Baggage Match (PPBM) should be carried out.

f. Thorough security check on catering, fuel and maintenance vehicles accessing the airside must be conducted.

In Dr. H. O. Demuren's 'Perspectives in Multi-Layer Aviation Security System & Passenger Facilitation' presentation paper, he explains: The directives stressed that all airlines are to ensure that any passenger that refuses to comply with 100% screening should be denied boarding. In addition, all foreign carriers and Nigeria carriers operating international routes have been directed to acquire EDS equipment to be used at secondary screening/boarding gate. This is now mandatory for all passengers on U.S. direct flights and those going via Europe.

Nigeria Government also signed a Memorandum of Understanding (MoU) with the Government of the Unites States of America for the reciprocal deployment of air marshals on aircraft bound to and coming from the United States to Nigeria. The MoU was signed in Washington DC, USA on 18th February 2010. And on the 08 June 2011, Nigeria signed the Agreement in Washington, DC. This also led to Nigeria establishing a separate and dedicated screening bay for all United States bound direct flight at our international airports of Lagos and Abuja.

## GAPS AND OUR EXPERIENCE

On December 25, 2009, Umar Farouk Abdulmutallab, a 23-year- old Nigerian citizen, was alleged to have attempted to detonate an improvised explosive device (IED), which he managed to smuggle onboard the Northwest Flight 253.[41] Farouk had paid $2,831 in cash for his Lagos-Amsterdam-Detroit return ticket with a return date that was booked for January 8, 2010.[42] The international flight – an Airbus A330-323E - had just taken off from the Amsterdam Airport at Schiphol, Amsterdam in the Netherlands, and was headed for the Detroit Metropolitan Wayne County Airport in the United States. The incident, which was branded "a failed Christmas Day al- Qaeda bombing attempt," saw Farouk attempt to set off a plastic/chemical explosive that was sewn to his underwear; which would have been disastrous for all 290 individuals on board to become the deadliest civil aviation incident on US soil. The explosive had failed to detonate properly, before Jasper Schuringa, a Dutch passenger, tackled Farouk and restrained him; while other passengers on board assisted with putting out a small fire that had erupted in the process. The pilot was able to land the aircraft safely with no fatalities to passengers and crew on board while Abdulmutallab was arrested, handcuffed, and detained by ground law enforcement officials. The suspected terrorist was convicted of attempted murder and attempting to use a weapon of mass destruction on board a U.S. civil / commercial aircraft, amongst other criminal charges. He was sentenced to life in prison without the possibility of parole, and is currently incarcerated at the ADX Florence Supermax prison, near Florence, Colorado.[43]

Consequently, The U.S. President, Barack Obama ordered an investigation into the incident, describing the failure of the United States to prevent the bombing attempt as "totally unacceptable," and citing critical "human and systemic failures."[44] The U.S. Secretary of Homeland Security, Janet Napolitano, is said to have admitted that the system "failed miserably" in preventing Abdulmutallab from boarding the aircraft with an explosive device;[45] even though prior to the attack, the U.S. had received intelligence regarding a powder-bomb-planned attack by a Yemen- based Nigerian man. In the aftermath of this incident, several civil aviation experts and stakeholders have continued to decry and criticize the existence of deep-running vulnerabilities and technical loopholes in the TSA's layered security management approach.

It was revealed in a June 2015 report that classified covert tests for vulnerability assessment of the TSA layered security framework, which were carried out by the Department of Homeland Security's (DHS) Office of Inspector General at security checkpoints at various airports in the United States, discovered that TSA officers and equipment were unable to detect simulated weapons and threat situations for over 90% of the time.[46]

A number of incidents in the experiences of civil aviation in Nigeria lend credence to the findings of this report that led to the resignation of the acting head of TSA, and resulted in extensive revisions of the TSA layered security framework by the DHS. Asides the fact that Umar Farouk Abdulmutallab is reported to have departed from the Murtala Muhammed International Airport (MMIA) on Christmas Eve of December 2009 at about 23:00 hours on board KLM Flight 588 – a Boeing 777 headed for Schiphol Airport in Amsterdam,[47] ostensibly already in possession of the explosive device; the case of Miss Zainab Aliyu and Mr. Ibrahim Abubakar presents another recent example.

All these incidents reveal that coordinated mechanisms of action by nefarious crime syndicates and cartels could be able to subvert and outwit multiple layers of the TSA security framework and almost-entirely compromise security in ways that could literally result in the death of innocent, unsuspecting travelers. Perhaps, effective intelligence gathering might have earlier helped to bust the activities of the drug cartel that sought to implicate Zainab and Ibrahim, as well as revealed earlier the ties that Umar Farouk Abdulmutallab had with the Al-Qaeda terrorists' organization. Trained canine units at the airport might have also been able to sniff out drugs and contraband substances as they were being passed around the airport premises by members of the drug cartel as well as explosives that might have been strapped to the body or packed in baggage. The effective presence and alertness of transportation security inspectors and bomb appraisal officers might have also helped to prevent the planting of an unknown, unchecked, and uncleared baggage on the unsuspecting Zainab Aliyu and Ibrahim Abubakar at the airport, as well as preventing Farouk Abdulmutallab from leaving a secured port of exit to board a commercial aircraft with explosives strapped to his body. Random employee screenings might have also helped to fish out malicious members and criminal syndicates from among airport and airline staff and employees. These are just to highlight a few of the ways by which an effective application of the TSA's layered security management approach might have helped to forestall these two incidents that basically amounted to a national embarrassment to the nations involved.

## SUBMISSION FOR A PROGRESSIVE SECURITY MANAGEMENT

I can say, without fear of contradiction, that the state of security in various domestic and international airports around Nigeria should be a source of concern for any discerning mind. Issues ranging from various reported complaints of begging,[48] extortion,[49] bribery,[50] hooliganism, thuggery,[51] luggage theft and pilfering,[52], [53]advanced fee fraud, and impersonation, to several other ostensible allegations of sexual and other forms of harassment, bullying, as well as systemic violations of fundamental human rights, have been documented through media reports as well as formal complaints filed with law enforcement agencies. Unfortunately, these have not received the urgent attention of government. These acts continue with reckless abandon at several airports around the country.

Apparently, the presence of these vices continues to create conducive havens for criminal activities at domestic and international airports in Nigerian; a lot of illegality typically thrive in disorderliness, and I have never known our airports to be as orderly as it should be. This situation creates critical vulnerabilities for aviation security management which could run right from the airport through the entry ports and border protection, onto aircrafts and into international airspaces.

The first step towards development is order, thus, the first and most important step to robust and effective aviation security management would be for federal aviation management authorities to clear out airports of the criminal elements parading themselves within the environs; only then would it be possible to establish, sustain, and propagate efficient security management mechanisms in line with the recommendations of the TSA's layered security management approach.

Ultimately, security management that would prove, and continue to prove effective and efficient in dealing with contemporary threats, would remain a journey and never a destination. There will never be a time to rest on the oars, as the threat landscape continues to evolve. By listening to stakeholders, conducting periodic reviews, audits, and assessments of security structures, and constructs, as well as scheduled maintenance of relevant security infrastructure, it can be possible to sustain the continuous journey to a better security management for the Nigerian aviation industry.

You will remember I have talked about the fact that risk is a part of life but we are able to do certain things to make life less perilous - things like avoiding unnecessary risks. Doing all that is possible to ensure the safety and security of travelers is the best way of cutting costs without cutting corners. The reason is not farfetched: people will rather travel long distances using the safest means available and the airplane remains that means.

# EPILOGUE

# WHAT IS COST CUTTING?

Cost cutting or reduction is a term used to describe actions taken by a firm to reduce costs and increase profits. Typically, cost-cutting tactics are implemented when a company is in financial difficulties or when the economy is experiencing a downturn.

**WHAT DOES IT MEAN TO CUT CORNERS?**
Generally, cutting corners means to do something in the easiest or shortest way possible, especially at the expense of high or even basic standards. Alternatively, and for the purpose of this book, you could say to cut corners means to act unlawfully. Cutting corners by not rigorously performing scheduled aviation maintenance, for example, is clearly plotting an ACCIDENT, and if the accountant cuts corners, the auditors will undoubtedly discover it. Of course, cutting costs is easier said than done. Here are some innovative strategies to reduce specific types of spending without jeopardizing your company's viability.

According to Bethany K. Lawrence, there are smart ways of cutting costs and they include the following:
- Eliminate discretionary spending.
- Buy more carefully.
- Look for cheaper credit card processing services.
- Stop paying for equipment you don't need.
- Renegotiate your lease or move.
- Sublet unneeded space.
- Cut employee perks.

Let me elaborate on three of the above listed.

**DISCRETIONARY SPENDING SHOULD BE ELIMINATED**
Wait before painting your building, purchasing new equipment, or adding additional personnel. You should proceed only if a specific expense is required to carry out a critical marketing or diversification strategy. Even if you've agreed to spend money under the terms of a contract, you can try to back out.

**PURCHASE WITH CAUTION**
Every firm makes purchases. It should go without saying that buying in lesser quantities and negotiating cheaper pricing can help you save money. However, because prices tend to fall as volume increases, combining both goals may appear unachievable.

When times are tight and suppliers are desperate for business, you'll be astonished at how many will decrease their pricing if you ask and refuse to accept no for an answer. Do not sign a long- term contract with the first vendor who provides you with a better bargain. If a competitor offers you a cheaper price, the vendor you already use will most likely try to keep your business by lowering the price even more.

**STOP SPENDING MONEY ON EQUIPMENT YOU DON'T REQUIRE** It's easy to commit to buying or leasing expensive equipment- trucks, automobiles, bulldozers, electronic equipment, forklifts, and so on-when things are good. Examine everything you own, particularly anything you're still paying for. Everything you don't need should be sold. Even if you sell a jet for less than you owe and have to make up the difference to pay off the loan, you'll usually save a lot of money in the long run. And if you only use it sometimes, you can probably hire it by the day for a lot less. If your company is losing money, your real estate may be your most important asset so make sure it is earning as much as it can. You can even consider moving your company to a different location and renting out the entire building. Be inventive. Even historically, strongly competitive retailers may be able to survive by merging office, warehouse, and even minor manufacturing operations in the same location.

## REDUCE YOUR PAY, AS WELL AS THAT OF HIGH-PAID EMPLOYEES

For many small firms, payroll is the most expensive expense. If this is the case for your company, decreasing other expenses will not be enough to bring in the savings your struggling company requires. You'll need to minimize the amount of your payroll sooner or later, and the sooner the better.

When circumstances are tough and jobs are scarce, it is common to be able to reduce wages by a modest percentage without losing staff. If you work for the corporation, you should be the first to receive a pay decrease (and if your spouse works for the business, both of you).

Even if your pay is already modest and decreasing it won't save much, cutting your own income will draw employees' attention and respect in ways that a dozen terrible financial forecasts won't.

## REDUCE THE WORK-WEEK

Cutting the work week is another method to share the economic pain while conserving jobs. Going to a four-and-a-half-day work, week, for example, saves 10% of payroll; a four-day week saves 20%.

Putting a stop to overtime hours would also save you money. The move will not considerably affect productivity if your staff are highly motivated to see your company through to better times (and appreciate the fact that the cuts avoid or limit layoffs). People will realize that in order to keep your business afloat, they'll have to work a little harder and smarter to get the same amount of work done in less time. A few employees may go, but in a down economy, the majority will prefer to keep what they have.

## LAY OFF WORKERS
Cutting jobs and letting go of long-term workers is never a pleasant thought. However, for many organizations where payroll is the largest expense, it is the only practical way to save money. A CEO in the corporate sector can order 10,000 job layoffs without ever meeting the people who will be laid off. However, shrinking a small company necessitates the agonizing chore of laying off people you know well and are friendly with. It is so difficult that some executives would prefer to watch their company collapse than take the axe. However, in order to exist, you must embrace the fact that your obligation to your employees is constrained by economic realities. Remember, you recruited staff in the hopes of making a profit, not to pay them indefinitely.

## INCREASE YOUR MARKETING EFFORTS WHILE LOWERING YOUR COSTS
When sales decline, you must expand your marketing efforts. However, investing for pricey advertising or other high-cost approaches is rarely cost-effective. Instead, your cash-saving plan should usually entail reducing traditional marketing spending and relying on low-cost guerilla marketing tactics which, among other things, seeks the support of your devoted consumers in rescuing your company.

**REDUCE THE NUMBER OF BUSINESS TRIPS**

If your company still requires a substantial quantity of travel, reduce it by at least half. Simply committing to this will drive you to concentrate on removing the least profitable half of your business.

**REDUCE EXPENSES ON INSURANCE**

When you're in a tight financial situation, the last thing you want to do is forego important insurance coverage for fire, theft, and liability. However, you may be able to lower your overall expenses by raising deductibles and dropping less important coverage for things like business disruption or the death of a key employee. If your company is established as an LLC or corporation, it makes more sense to save money on insurance than if you are a lone proprietor or partner who is personally liable for business losses.

Dr. Gabriel Gbenga Olowo – 2021.
**Internet Materials**

# REFERENCE

1. Norin, A. (2008). Airport Logistics– Modelling and Optimizing the Turn-Around Process. ISBN 978-91-7393-744-3.
2. Retrieved from https://www.diva-portal.org/smash/get/diva2:133720/FULLTEXT01.pdf
3. Zhang, Yao, J. J., & Hu, H. Q. (2013). The issues and strategies of air cargo service Chain in China. *China Transportation Review*, 2013(1), 22-28.
4. Wei, R. (2008). Features and the current situation of aviation logistics service Chain. Logistics Technology, 27(1): 23-40. 24International Civil Aviation Logistics and Management, Master. Retrieved from https://www.mastersportal.com/studies/149273/international-civil-aviation-logistics-and- management.html
5. Feng, D. M. (2015). Study on the formation mechanism of aviation logistics airport economic zone. Port Economy, 2(2015): 35-37.
6. Long, D. International Logistics: Global Supply Chain Management. Available at : www2.nkfust.edu.tw/~translab/globalLogisticsManagement/chapter08-v2.pdf
7. Feng, D. M. (2015). Study on the formation mechanism of aviation logistics airport economic zone. Port Economy, 2(2015): 35-37.
8. Wei, R. (2008). Features and the current situation of aviation logistics service Chain. Logistics Technology, 27(1): 23-40.
9. Norin, A. (2008). Airport Logistics - Modeling and Optimizing the Turn-Around Process. ISBN 978-91-7393-744-3. Retrieved from https://www.diva-portal.org/smash/get/diva2:133720/FULLTEXT01.pdf

10. Kim, C. and Barnhart, C. (2007). Flight schedule design for a charter airline. Computers and Operations research, vol. 34, pp. 1516-1531.
11. Sarac, A., Batta, R, and Rump, C, M, (2006). A branch-and-price approach for operational aircraft maintenance routing. European Journal of Operation Research, vol. 175, pp.1850-1869.
12. Barnhart, C., Cohn, A. M., Johnson, E. L., Klabjan, D., Nemhauser, G. L., and Vance, P, H, (2003). Airline Crew Scheduling. In Hall, R, W, ed., Handbook of Transportation Science, 2nd ed., Kluwer Academic Publishers.
13. International Civil Aviation Logistics and Management, Master.Retrieved from www.mastersportal.com/studies/149273/international-civil-aviation-logistics-and management.html
14. Luftfartsstyrelsen. ( 2008 ). Retrieved from http:// www.luftfartsstyrelsen.se
15. Norin, A. (2008). Airport Logistics– Modeling and Optimizing the Turn-Around Process. ISBN 978-91-7393-744-3. Retrieved from https://www.diva-portal.org/smash/get/diva2:133720/FULLTEXT01.pdf
16. Zhang, Yao, J. J. and Hu, H. Q. (2013). The issues and strategies of air cargo service Chain in China. China Transportation Review, 2013(1): 22-28.
17. Norin, A. (2008). Airport Logistics– Modeling and Optimizing the Turn-Around Process. ISBN 978-91-7393-744-3. Retrieved from https://www.diva-portal.org/smash/get/diva2:133720/FULLTEXT01.pdf
18. Zhang, Yao, J. J. and Hu, H. Q. (2013). The issues and strategies of air cargo service in China. China Transportation Review. (1): 22-28.

19. Zhang, Yao, J. J. and Hu, H. Q. (2013). The issues and strategies of air cargo service Chain in China. China Transportation Review, 2013(1): 22-28.
20. Qian, Q. (2008). Design and research of SAL logistics joint marketing platform. Shanghai Jiaotong University: Shanghai. 41 Zhang, Yao, J. J. and Hu, H. Q. (2013). The issues and strategies of air cargo service Chain in China. China Transportation. (1): 22-28.
21. Kao, C., Hu, H. Kung, B. and Hsieh, W. (2019). Strategic Planning for the Aviation Logistics Service Supply Chain in China. Business Management and Economics Research. ISSN(e): 2412- 1770, ISSN(p): 2413-855X. 5(1),1

# JOURNALS

Akpoghomeh, O. (1999), "The development of air transportation in Nigeria," *Journal of Transport Geography,* Vol. 7.

Ciesluk, K. (2000), How aircraft leasing works and why airlines do it? Retrieved from:
https://www.google.com/url?sa=t&rct=j&q=&esrc=s&source=we b&cd=&cad=rja&uact=8&ved=2ahU KEwiKtJqEssrqAhWFyoUKHad3BJMQFjAKegQIARAB&url= h ttps%3A%2F%2Fsimpleflying.com%2Fhow-aircraft-leasingworks%2F&usg=AOvVaw0nPMyzC40qxVK1oGo8iXdD

Energymix Report. (2019). Nigerian airlines urge FG to reduce the cost of aviation fuel, others. Retrieved from https://www.energymixreport.com/nigerian-airlines-urge-fg-to- reduce-cost-of-aviation-fuel-others/

Eze, C. (2017) Why running an airline is expensive in Nigeria. *THISDAYLive online.* Retrieved from https://www.thisdaylive.com/index.php/2017/06/09/why-running-an-airline-is- expensive-in-nigeria

Hadejia, K. (2018). Aviation unions: Is NCAA compromised? *The Eagle Online.*

Ihekwoaba, C. (2018). Saving Nigeria"s aviation sector. *THE NERVE AFRICA online.*

Retrieved from https://thenerveafrica.com/13695/saving-nigerias-aviation-sector/

KGAL Group. (2016). Aircraft leasing - A promising investment market for institutional investors. Retrieved from www.kgal-group.com

Lawani, M. (2019,). Aviation challenges: Expert cautions over Nigeria operations (An interview of Mr Herbert Odika). *Vanguard Newspaper*. Retrieved from https://www.vanguardngr.com/2019/01/aviation-challenges-expert-cautions-over-nigeria- operations/

Okunbor, K. O. (2017). Cutting costs through local aircraft maintenance. *THE NATION online*. Retrieved from https://thenationonlineng.net/cutting-costs-local-aircraft-maintenance/

McCormick, M. (2017). What is Profit Maximisation? Retrieved from www.https%3A%2F%2Fblog.blackcurve.com%2Fwhat-is-profit-maximisation&usg=AOvVaw1sopTuLo5CPzzpaAl9_AFF

Dr. H. O. Demuren (2022) Perspectives In Multi-Layer Aviation Security System & Passenger Facilitation https://skylibrarys.files.wordpress.com/2016/07/annex-17-security.pdf

Wikipedia online Dictionary

# BOOKS

Adeeyo, A. (2017), Education for life. Unpublished lecture during 2017 Staff Colloquium in Adeleke University, Ede, Osun State.

Gambo, A.Z and Adebanjo, A. (2021). Developing security conscious mindset

# ABOUT THE BOOK

In Nigeria, the airline business may look appealing for investment, especially because of the fact that Nigeria as a country is blessed with the biggest domestic aviation market on the continent of Africa. However, the business has thrived better in many smaller markets because of stakeholders' commitment to playing the game strictly according to the rules while eschewing cutting corners in those other countries. The huge opportunities in this market that ordinarily should have made airline businesses in Nigeria lucrative, have not yet been properly harnessed for the benefit of investors and the country in general. Even though Nigerian airlines have been operating for years, they have not been able to hack the secret of successful airline business operations; and this may remain elusive if the focus is on cutting corners to cut costs. Thus, this book pinpoints the immediate and remote causes of the apparent inability of the aviation industry in Nigeria to effectively thrive with most of the causes oscillating around lack of understanding of the regulatory frameworks and rules which must not be circumvented in a bid to cut corners and cut costs. To achieve efficiency in the airline business and operate profitably, this book presents the dynamics that ensure optimum performance and safety with zero deviation from international regulatory frameworks in the airline business.

# ABOUT THE AUTHOR

Dr. Gabriel O. Olowo is veteran aviation economist and currently the president of Aviation Safety Round Table Initiative (ART) since 2015.

He began his aviation career as a management trainee with Lufthansa German Airlines in 1975 after a brief stint in 1973 as Flight Dispatcher Trainee with Nigeria Airways Limited.

Olowo has since then, served in various capacities such as assistant manager with Lufthansa Airlines; deputy general manager with Varig Brazilian Airline; and executive director at Bellview Airlines Limited. Olowo has had an uninterrupted career of approximately 50 years in commercial aviation, revenue management, airport facilitation, Slot management, airline training, spares sourcing, maintenance and repair, safety and security and aircraft acquisition. An alumnus of the University of Lagos where he obtained his first degree in business administration and an M.Sc. in economics (manpower planning), Olowo acquired doctorate degrees awarded by Samuel Adegboyega University, Ogwa, Nigeria, in business administration, and Escae University, Cotonou, Republic of Benin in technology.

Olowo has served on several groups, committees, and panels, including the Ministerial Committee on Restructuring of Nigeria Airways Limited in September 2001 and the Ministerial Technical Committee on the Establishment of a new Flag Carrier in August 2003. He has also served as chairman of the IATA Agency Investigation Panel (A.I.P) for West Africa and a member of the ECOWAS Parliament Committee on Implementation of the Yamoussoukro Treaty.

Olowo has attended several professional training courses across the world and he is the current chairman of Sabre West & Central Africa (CWA), the world's largest software innovative technology provider for airlines and travel trade.

A member of the Nigeria/U.S. Chamber of Commerce, Olowo has consistently supported Nigeria / US business development and exchange of commerce.

Dr. Gabriel Olowo is the founder and chairman of InterGuide Group of Companies, (InterGuide Air, InterGuide Academy, Sabre Global Technology-West Africa, GolfView Suites and Conference Centre (IASG). He is a member, Board of Trustees (BOT) of Ikeja Golf Club, Lagos.

Dr. Olowo's extensive aviation experience has made him an acknowledged expert in airline and aviation business management. He has provided varied consultancy services in these areas and is an author of many aviation industry related publications.

Olowo is the first African to pioneer an aviation management curriculum at any university when Sabre Global Technology Limited, West Africa, partnered with Babcock University for an MBA programme in airline studies since 2018. The study is aimed at producing employable human resources for aviation leaders.

Olowo is a fellow of the Nigerian Institute of Management (FNIM), a fellow of the Institute of Tourism Professional (FITP), a member of the American Chamber of Commerce, Nigeria- Brazil Chamber of Commerce and Industry, British Chamber of Commerce and Osun Development Board.

Dr. Gabriel O. Olowo, a seasoned golfer, is married to Deaconess Stella Olubisi Olowo for upwards of 40 years and their marriage is blessed with children and grandchildren.

# REFERENCE

[1] Aljazeera (November 28, 2018). Pilots struggled with flightsystems in Indonesia crash. Retrieved from: https://www.aljazeera.com/news/2018/11/pilots-struggled- flight- systems-indonesia-crash-181128013738564.html. Accessed on November 28, 2018.

[2] Guardian News (November 28, 2018). Lion Air jet was not airworthy on flight before crash, Indonesia investigators say. Retrieved from: https://www.theguardian.com/world/2018/nov/28/lion-air-jet-was- not-airworthy-on- flight-before-crash-indonesia- investigators-say. Accessed on November 28, 2018.

[3] Assembly Resolution A36-13, Appendix A. ICAO Doc 9902, Assembly Resolutions in force as of 28 September 2007. Retrieved March 04, 2019 from https://www.icao.int/ environmental-protection/Documents/A36_Res22_Prov.pdf

[4] ICAO SARPs - Standards and Recommended Practices. Retrieved March 04, 2019 from https://www.icao.int/safety/safetymanagement/pages/sarps.aspx

[5] Cabin Operations Safety: Best Practices Guide (3rd Edition). Retrieved March 04, 2019 from https://skybrary.aero/bookshelf/books/3996.pdf

[6] Annex 19: Safety Management – ICAO. Retrieved March 04, 2019 from https://www.icao.int/safety/SafetyManagement/WebsiteDesignJuly2016/Flyer_US-Letter_ANB-ANNEX19-SM_2016-10-03.AP.pdf

[7] Safety. Retrieved March 04, 2019 from https://www.iata.org/whatwedo/safety/Pages/index.aspx

[8] Best Industry Practices for Aircraft Decommissioning (BIPAD). Retrieved March 04, 2019 from https://www.iata.org/publications/Documents/BIPAD.pdf

[9] Aircraft Reliability Guidelines. Retrieved March 04, 2019 from https://www.iata.org/publications/store/Pages/aircraft- reliability-guidelines.aspx

[10] Best Practices Guide for Cabin Retrofit and EIS. Retrieved March 04, 2019 from https://www.iata.org/publications/ D o c u m e n t s / Best_practices_guide_Cabin_retrofit_and_EIS_Ed 1.pdf

[11] Aljazeera (November 28, 2018). Pilots struggled with flight systems in Indonesia crash. Retrieved from: https://www.aljazeera.com/news/2018/11/pilots-struggled-flight-systems-indonesia-crash-181128013738564.html. Accessed on November 28, 2018.

[12] MSN News (March 12, 2019). Senior captain who piloted downed Ethiopian plane has connections to Calgary. Retrieved from: https://www.msn.com/en-ca/news/canada/ senior-captain-who-piloted-downed-ethiopian-plane-has- connections-to-calgary/ar-BBUEsla. Accessed on March 18, 2019.

[13] New York Times (March 10, 2019). Victims of Ethiopian Airlines Flight 302 Came From at Least 30 Nations. Retrieved from: https://www.nytimes.com/2019/03/10/ world/africa/ethiopian-airlines-plane-crash-victims.html. Accessed on March 18, 2019.

[14] Guardian News (March 14, 2019). Why has Boeing pulled its 737 Max fleet – and what took it so long?. Retrieved from: https://www.theguardian.com/business/2019/mar/14/why- has-

boeing-pulled-its-737-max-fleet-potentially-fatal-safety- flaw. Accessed on March 18, 2019.

[15] CNN (March 17, 2019). After two fatal Boeing plane crashes, the world turned on the US. Retrieved from: https:// www.cnbc.com/2019/03/17/two-boeing-737-fatal-plane- crashes-the-world-turns-on-the-faa.html. Accessed on March 18, 2019.

[16] CNN (March 13, 2019). Pilots complained about the 737 Max in a federal database. Retrieved from: https:// edition.cnn.com/2019/03/13/us/pilot-complaints-boeing-737-max/index.html. Accessed on March 18, 2019.

[17] New York Times (February 03, 2019). After a Lion Air 737 Max Crashed in October, Questions about the Plane Arose. Retrieved from: https://www.nytimes.com/ 2019/02/03/world/asia/lion-air-plane-crash-pilots.html. Accessed on March 18, 2019.

[18] Aligbe, C. (June 30, 2016). Aviation regulation in Nigeria: The chequered history. Retrieved from Africa Travel News: http://www.atqnews.com/ng/africa-aviation-regulation- nigeria-chequered-history/. Accessed on March 18, 2019.

[19] Ogala, E. (March 10, 2019). 10 worst plane crashes involving Nigeria. Retrieved from Premium T i m e s Nigeria: https://www.premiumtimesng.com/news/5556-ten_worst_plane_crashes_involving_nigeria.html. Accessed on March 18, 2019.

[20] Nigerian Civil Aviation Authority (NCAA) Website: About Us. NCAA Responsibilities. Retrieved from http:// ncaa.gov.ng/about-ncaa/ncaa-responsibilities/. Accessed on April 01, 2019.

[21] Wurster, J.F. (1980). Causes and Nature of Injuries in Air Accidents. In: Frey R., Safar P. (eds) Types and Events of Disasters

Organization in Various Disaster Situations. Disaster Medicine. Vol 1. Springer, Berlin, Heidelberg

[22] Tenerife airport disaster. (1977). Retrieved from https://ipfs.io/ i p f s / QmXoypizjW3WknFiJnKLwHCnL72vedxjQkDDP1mXWo 6uco/wiki/Tenerife_airport_disaster.html

[23] 11 Devastating Plane Crashes Caused By Pilot Error. Available at: https://www.lolwot.com/11-devastating-plane- crashes-caused-by-pilot-error/

[24] Punch Newspaper. (2019). State govt orders relocation of market close to Enugu Airport. Available at: https://punchng.com/state-govt-orders-relocation-of-market-close- to-enugu-airport.

[25] Morris, J. (2015). What is the safest way to travel? One chart which reveals that flying is less dangerous than you may think. Retrieved from www.cityam.com/215834/one-chart- showing-safest-ways-travel

[26] Wurster, J.F. (1980). Causes and Nature of Injuries in Air Accidents. In: Frey R., Safar P. (eds) Types and Events of Disasters Organization in Various Disaster Situations. Disaster Medicine, vol 1. Springer, Berlin, Heidelberg

[27] Gambrell, J. (2012). Rains Slow Search in Nigeria Plane Crash. Time. Associated Press. Archived from the original on 5 June 2012. Available at: https://en.wikipedia.org/wiki/ Dana_Air_Flight_992

[28] AsianNews.it. (2018): US sanctions have turned Iranian airplanes into $flying coffins". Available at: http:// www.asianews.it/news-en/-US-sanctions-have-turned- Iranian-airplanes-into-flying-coffins-43184.html

[29] McFadden, M. and Worrells, D. S. 2012: Global Outsourcing of Aircraft Maintenance. Journal of Aviation Technology and

Engineering 1:2 63–73DOI: 10.5703/1288284314659. Available online at http://docs.lib.purdue.edu/jate. Accessed May 9, 2019.

[30] Moody, E. (2010, November 1). Southeast Asia special: Dynamic demands Overhaul and Maintenance. Retrieved from http://www.aviationweek. com / aw / generic/ story_generic.jsp?channel5om&id5news/om/2010/11/01/ OM_11_01_2010_p22-260993.xml&headline5null&next510

[31] Kley, S. (2016). Aircraft Line Maintenance – Mobile Ways of Communication. Retrieved from: www.inform software.com/blog/post/aircraft-line-maintenance-mobile- ways-of-communication

[32] Caldwell, M. (2012). Nigerian opposition links air crash to corruption. Available at: https://www.dw.com/en/nigerian-opposition-links-air-crash-to-corruption/a-16001839

[33] Onyekakeyah, L. (2001).Nigeria: A Requiem for Nigeria Air. Available at: https://allafrica.com/stories/20180 9250130.html

[34] Torulagha, P. S. (2006). The Effects of Corruption on Commercial Aviation and Land Transportation in Nigeria. Available at: https://nigeriaworld.com/articles/2006/ jan/060.html

[35] Business Dictionary. Innovation. Retrieved from: http:// www.businessdictionary.com/definition/innovation.html. Accessed on April 26, 2019.

[36] Harris, W. How Autopilot Works: Autopilots and Avionics. Retrieved from How Stuff Works– Science: https://science.howstuffworks.com/transport/flight/modern/ autopilot1.htm. Accessed on April 26, 2019.

[37] Osa-Okunbor, K. (2015, September 08). Government should assist domestic airlines with incentives. Retrieved from The Nation

Online: https://thenationonlineng.net/govt-should- assist-domestic-airlines-with-incentives/. Accessed on April 26, 2019.

[38] Nosike, M. (2015, September 12). NAHCO deploys new 1.5Billion Naira equipment across Nigerian airports. Retrieved from The Vanguard Newspaper Online: https://www.vanguardngr.com/2015/09/nahco-deploys-new-1-5billion-naira-equipment-across-nigerian-airports/. Accessed on April 26, 2019.

[39] Okoroafor, C. (2015, September 08). Aviation in Nigeria: The transformation that Nigerian airports need. Retrieved from Ventures Africa: http://venturesafrica.com/the- need-to- transform-the-nigerian-airports/. Accessed on April 26, 2019.

[40] Sleeping in Airports. Worst Airports of 2017: Top 5 Worst Airports in Africa. Retrieved from: https://www.sleepinginairports.net/survey/2017-worst-airports-complete- results.htm#africa. Accessed on April 26, 2019.

[41] Kair, L. (June 09, 2010). A layered approach to security. Retrieved from International Airport Review: https://www.internationalairportreview.com/article/2563/a-layered-approach- to-security/. Accessed on April 26, 2019.

[42] Mason, J. (January 01, 2010). Obama summons intelligence chiefs for security talks. Retrieved from Reuters: https://www.reuters.com/article/us-security-airline/obama- summons-intel-chiefs-for -security-talks- idUSTRE5BU3NZ20100101. Accessed on April 26, 2019.

[43] Bunkley, N. (February 16, 2012). Would-Be Plane Bomber Is Sentenced to Life in Prison. Retrieved from The New York Times:https://www.nytimes.com/2012/02/17/us/would-be- plane-bomber-sentenced-to-life.html. Accessed on April 26, 2019.

[44] Allen, N. (December 29, 2009). Barack Obama admits 'unacceptable systemic failure' in Detroit plane attack. Retrieved from The Daily Telegraph (UK): https://www. telegraph.co.uk/news/worldnews/barackobama/6908709/ Barack-Obama-admits-unacceptable-systemic-failure-in-\Detroit-plane-attack.html. Accessed on April 26, 2019.

[45] Charles, D. (December 28, 2009). System to keep air travel safe failed: Napolitano. Retrieved from Reuters: https:// www. reuters . com / article / us - security - airline napolitano/ system-to-keep-air-travel-safe-failed-napolitano- idUSTRE5BQ0Z420091228. Accessed on April 26, 2019.

[46] Johnstone, W. (October 06, 2015). Passenger Aviation Security Layers. Retrieved from SciTech Connect – Physical Security & Emergency Management: http://scitechconnect. elsevier.com/passenger-aviation-security-layers/.Accessed on April 26, 2019.

[47] Shane, S., & Lipton, E. (December 26, 2009). Passengers' Quick Action Halted Attack. Retrieved from The New York Times : https://www.nytimes.com/2009/12/27/us/ 27plane.html. Accessed on April 26, 2019.

[48] Falade, T. (December 01, 2018). Begging, Extortion at Nigerian Airports. Retrieved from Independent Newspapers Nigeria: https://www.independent.ng/begging-extortion-at- nigerian-airports/. Accessed on April 26, 2019.

[49] Oladeinde O. (November 04, 2018). INVESTIGATION: At Lagos airport, officials still extort travelers (1). Retrieved from Premium Times: https:// www.premiumtimesng.com/news/headlines/294017-at-lagos- airport-officials-still- extort-travellers.html. Accessed on April 26, 2019.

[50] Aluko, O. (December 12, 2016). Travelers give bribes at airports – ICPC. Retrieved from Punch Newspapers Online: https://punchng.com/travellers-give-bribes-airports-icpc/. Accessed on April 26, 2019.

[51] Ekwealor, V. (March 25, 2019). Begging, Extortion at Nigerian Airports. Retrieved from TechPoint Africa: https://techpoint.africa/2019/03/25/nigerian-airport-authority- fighting-online-hailing-taxi-services/. Accessed on April 26, 2019.

[52] Soyombo, F. (November 27, 2017). Checked-in luggage thieves at Ethiopian Airlines and Nigerian airports. Retrieved from The Cable News: https://www.thecable. ng/ checked-luggage-thieves-ethiopian-airlines-nigerian-airports. Accessed on April 26, 2019.

[53] Ihua-Maduenyi, M. (December 05, 2016). Passengers grumble over rising luggage theft at airports. Retrieved from The Punch Newspapers Online: https://punchng.com/ passengers-grumble-rising-luggage-theft-airports/. Accessed on April 26, 2019.